# Good Taste

A Guide to Northern Michigan Cuisine

by

Patty LaNoue Stearns

Arbutus Press
P.O. Box 234
Mayfield, Michigan 49666
Arbutuspress@traverse.com
www.Arbutuspress.com

Library of Congress Data-in-Publication available

ISBN 0-9665316--6-3

10 9 8 7 6 5 4 3 2 1

Printed in the United States of America

First Edition

Cover photo by Dietrich Floeter
www.dietrichfloeter.com

# Contents

Introduction

Section One
Restaurant Reviews - Alphabetical     9

Section Two
Northern Michigan's Best Bets     135

Artisan Bread     136
Burger Blitz     137
Cheese     139
Cheesecake     140
Cherry Festival Food     141
Cherry and Other Fruit Products     143
Chocolate Tour     144
Coffeehouses/Delis/Cafes     145
Designer Milk     148
Farm Markets     149
Ice Cream     152
Foodie Heaven     154
Pies     157
Pizza     158
Wineries     159

Section Three
My Fave Foodie Spots by Location     163

Index     171

# Introduction

As a kid growing up in the Detroit area, I took regular treks with my family to the North Country. We toured the attractions, hung out on the sand dunes, splashed in the crystal waters and checked out the little shops and interesting eateries that characterize this part of the world. But we never had enough time to see or taste everything. I always longed to linger, just a few more hours, a few more days, a few more weeks.

Then I married a man who felt the same way. On our first foray to Traverse City 20 years ago, we vowed we'd move here someday — despite a hotel room with funky brown shag walls and a scary red velvet bedspread. The hotel shall remain nameless — it's still here, presumably redecorated—but we still laugh about the place every time we drive by.

Joe and I took the big plunge in 1999. We are no longer Fudgies. We are living the dream. He's making handcrafted furniture and I'm writing about the things I love. Not only have we relocated to some of the most beautiful surroundings imaginable, we have come at a pivotal time—the restaurant scene is starting to sizzle. What 20 years ago was a bastion of mainly middle-of-the-road dining with a handful of fine restaurants is now rife with culinary possibilities. Everywhere there are more and more year-round dining spots with ambitious menus, world-class chefs, laid-back dress codes and lovely views. The accent is decidedly regional, with whitefish, asparagus, morel mushrooms and tart cherries appearing on most menus. There's also an emerging ethnic vibe—Mexican, Chinese, a bit of Thai, Japanese, Indian, French and Mediterranean flavors punctuate many menus—and our adventurous palates are pleading for more.

That's your cue, restaurateurs—bring it on.

This book will guide you to the eateries, gourmet grocers, bakeries, cooking schools, kitchen stores and other foodie haunts that I've discovered so far. Much of the following has appeared in the weekly dining column I write for the *Traverse City Record-Eagle*, called "Good Taste." Without the support and encouragement I've received from my astute editor, Kathy Gibbons, and my wonderful husband, Joe, who accompanied me during most of this two-year eating expedition, this book would not be possible.

I will take you through the high seasons, when the pace up north is bustling with the promise of all those blue skies, beaches, al fresco dining and the blaze of autumn leaves in fall. Then into winter, when life up north slows to a mellow roll and the snowy days look like the inside of a Christmas globe. That's when restaurant dining becomes a lazy, cozy event by a fire, often with a view of the bay, no-wait seating, attentive service and first-class food.

I'm not sure which season I like more. They're all pretty extraordinary up here in northern Michigan.

These reviews are strictly my opinion, and I have paid for all of my meals. If a restaurant is not listed, I've either not experienced it, haven't heard a vibe about it, or I've been there and feel it isn't worth including. In a few cases I have listed restaurants that I haven't visited, but because I've heard good things about the food, I've included them but left them unrated. I'm sure there are good places I've missed, but this is an ongoing project that will be updated frequently. Hey, I'm eating as fast as I can! Call ahead for hours and reservations, as many establishments are seasonal.

—Patty LaNoue Stearns

# Section One

# Restaurant Reviews

Dinner entree prices:
Inexpensive: under $10
Moderate: $10 to $20
Expensive: $20 and above

Rating:
✦✦Good
✦✦✦ Wonderful
✦✦✦✦Marvelous
✦✦✦✦✦The best

# Amical

La Cuisine Amical,
229 E. Front St.,
Traverse City,
231-941-8888 or
www.amical.com.
Lunch and dinner
Mon.-Sat. 11 a.m.-10
p.m., Sun. breakfast 9
a.m.-3 p.m.
Prices are moderate.
Rating ✦✦✦

On a dead-of-winter Friday night in downtown Traverse City, the *cognoscenti* came out in full force for a taste of the Naked Chef. The fireplace was blazing, drinks and laughter and conversation flowed like the steady unseasonable rain outside, and the menu was a marvelous mix of Asian and Mediterranean.

Amical, the fabulous Front Street bistro with the French accent and authentic accoutrements, was definitely the place to see and be seen. The occasion: one of its monthly Cookbook Series dinners, "The Naked Chef Takes Off," featuring the recipes of British wonder boy and Food Channel charmer Jamie Oliver. Amical's annual cookbook dinners, which have included recipes from Patricia Wells, Charlie Trotter and Ming Tsai, run from November to the second weekend in May. They keep the year-round restaurant filled with locals when the tourist trade ebbs, and Horizon Books next door carries each cookbook used in Amical's series for those who want to try the recipes at home.

I am partial to Amical for several reasons, service being one. Many of its servers and kitchen staff have been there for years, attesting to the convivial, family atmosphere the restaurant exudes. Owner Dave Denison was a sous chef at Hattie's in Sutton's Bay before opening Amical in July of '94. Chef Jon Eakes, a graduate of Northwestern Michigan College Culinary School, has titillated palates since January of 1996, when the restaurant got its beer and wine license and turned into a bistro.

Amical's regular menu features a well-composed wine list and a great selection of appetizers—the hot pastry twists stuffed with feta cheese and tapenade are my favorites. There are divine salads such as creamy apple-walnut with Gorgonzola with a nice lemon-olive oil dressing; and entrees like pasta, lamb, roasted chicken, salmon and shrimp, duck, and a tasty center-cut sirloin that is pan-seared and served with balsamic-brandy sauce and garlic mashed potatoes. I can't resist the raspberry crème brulee, one of several classic French pastries that seduce me when I walk past the display by the hostess area.

Amical gets my vote for the best people watching in town—especially from the patio on Front Street. It's positively Parisian.

# Andante

Bob Stark calls his stylish restaurant's menu a fusion of regional Michigan, American Southwest, classic European, Asian and Pacific Rim. Each year, when Andante reopens for the season, Stark unveils a completely new menu.

Andante, whose name implies—and delivers—elegant meals presented at a slow, smooth pace, sits at the perimeter of Petoskey's historic Gaslight District in an unassuming two-story former home. Inside, amid fresh flowers in vases, impressionistic art and stellar views of Little Traverse Bay, diners can take refuge in the calm, listening to soft music while supping on deliciously inventive fare.

Past dishes have included tequila-cured salmon quesadilla with wasabe crème fraiche, or a moist, perfectly grilled veal chop with roasted-garlic smashed purple potatoes. End your meal with a frozen mocha parfait with Baileys Irish Cream Anglaise.

# Apache Trout Grill

The view of West Grand Traverse Bay from the dining room is divine in this casual, rustic, always packed eatery, and so are the meaty ribs. My favorite item is the barbecued shrimp appetizer stuffed with horseradish and wrapped in bacon, enough for a meal. Pasta, seafood and salads punctuate the menu.

Apache Trout Grill,
13671 S. West Bay Shore,
Traverse City,
231-947-7079;
Hours:
Mon.-Thurs. 11-10,
Fri.-Sat. 11-11,
Sun. noon-9.
Full bar, private dock for customers.
Moderate.
Rating ✦✦

# Arcadia Bluffs

Arcadia Bluffs,
14710 Northwood
Hwy.,
Arcadia,
1-800-494-8666
or 231-889-3009
www.arcadiabluffs.com.
Hours, dining room
and deck: Lunch 11 a.m.-
4 p.m., dinner 4-10 p.m.
daily. Golfers Patio
Grill & Sunroom: Mon.
11 a.m.-sunset, Tues.-
Sun. 9 a.m.-sunset.
Moderate to expensive.

The 200-seat restaurant at this wide-open golf course offers sunset views over Lake Michigan from the dining room and deck, porch or veranda and menu items such as caribou with bacon, stuffed whitefish and bistecca ribeye steak with sunset mashed potatoes. No reservations, just a waiting list.

# Auntie Pasta's

Perhaps because of its less-than-authentic-sounding name, I never gave this place a thought until I found out my very Italian friend Ron eats there at least once a week. I checked it out. It was good, and for the price, authentic enough.

The setting's lively, fun and casual with an Italian-market theme. It's open and inviting, with a nice view of the Boardman River, and the small room called Zio's that diners pass to get into the main restaurant is a checkerboard-patterned delight that features pizza, subs, calzones, soup and salads.

Auntie Pasta's, Logan's Landing, 2030 South Airport, Traverse City, 231-941-8147. Open Mon.-Sat. 11 a.m.-10 p.m., Sun. noon-10 p.m.; Zio's: Mon.-Sat. 4-11 p.m., Sun. 4-11 p.m. Inexpensive to moderate. Rating ✦✦

Our bread, wrapped in red-and-white paper, was crusty, warm and fabulous, my Italian sausage with peppers, penne pasta and red sauce was tasty, and my husband's almond-crusted whitefish was dreamy. The menu offers daily specials, a host of pasta dishes as well as chicken, veal, beef, seafood, soups and salads. Which goes to show I can't judge a place by its name.

# La Bècasse

La Bècasse,
9001 S. Dunns Farm Rd.
on Glen Lake at the
corner of highways 616
and 675,
Burdickville,
231-334-3944. Dinners
begin at 6 p.m. Open
seven nights a week from
early May through the
third week in October,
then Christmas week and
Valentine's weekend.
Expensive.
Rating ✦✦✦✦

This cozy little 40-seat inn on Glen Lake, with its herb garden and fruit trees, would be right at home in the French countryside near Provence—which is exactly how Peachy and John Rentenbach felt when they first dined here.

"When you're downstate, you get the feeling that you might like to live someplace less complicated, more beautiful," says Grosse Pointe native Peachy, former test-kitchen director of the *Detroit Free Press*. So 15 years ago, the Rentenbachs bought the restaurant from its previous owner and moved to Burdickville to "live out the dream," as Peachy calls it — six months toiling 18-plus hours a day at the restaurant, and another six months traveling the world.

Part the velvet curtains at the entranceway and inhale the aroma of veal stock simmering in the kitchen—another hint that you're in for some fine French cooking. Chef Greg Murphy, who made his reputation downstate at Café Bon Homme in Plymouth, does the honors in the kitchen.

La Becasse is decorated simply with embroidered cotton batiste curtains that Peachy made herself, peasant chairs with straw seats, white tablecloths, bud vases filled with flowers from the garden, pretty tapestries and plates hung on the walls with images of the bird that is the restaurant's namesake—the woodcock.

Choose a bottle from the small but superb wine list, or try a tasty combo of fresh cherry juice with sparkling water and lime. The menu changes weekly along with the season, but guests might find a starter of smoked salmon, whitefish and cream cheese atop a crusty baguette. Follow this with a creamy, molded broccoli-spinach timbale or one of the daily fish specials; whitefish looms large, sautéed, baked and sauced. Perhaps a melt-in-your-mouth sautéed breast of chicken with crunchy potato crust sounds better, surrounded by a rich truffle demi-glace.

Save room for one of Peachy's profiteroles—miniature cream puffs filled with ice cream and topped with bittersweet chocolate sauce. They're worth the whole trip.

# The Bluebird

The Bluebird Restaurant & Bar,
101 River St.,
Leland,
231-256-9081.
Hours: Lunch and dinner Tues.-Sun. Brunch 10 a.m.-2 p.m. Closed Mon. Check hours in season. Prices: Moderate. Rating ✦✦✦

It's a place with a long past and a true community center that keeps northern folks sane during the long winters. One reason is their weekly ethnic feasts that run from the end of November through April.

Over the last 15 years the Bluebird's ethnic menu on Wednesday and Thursday nights has featured everything from wild game to tapas. Its regular menu includes fresh local fish, seafood, steaks and touches of Asia, India, California and New Orleans.

Boat builder Martin Telgard and his wife Leone opened the Bluebird in 1927 as a sandwich shop. Then son Jim and his wife Nancy took over and expanded the restaurant to its present 10,000 square feet. Today, a third generation of Telgards, Skip and wife Lynne, run the 180-seat restaurant with 100-seat bar.

On the evening we visited, the annual benefit party for the Leelanau Conservancy, complete with blues band, was going strong. We ate in a booth on the bar side, and the people-watching was wonderful. Our server juggled all the extra customers with pleasant professionalism, so we didn't mind a bit of a wait for our food.

First, a warm basket of rolls that included something rarely seen at dinnertime but nonetheless fabulous—cinnamon rolls, a forever tradition at the Bluebird. Our friend Richard had the best thing on the menu–a sweet, fresh, lightly fried, delicate, well-textured plate of perch. The jalapeno-stuffed shrimp wrapped in bacon were smothered in too much barbecue sauce, but my husband's T-bone with

Argentinean chimichurra sauce was enormous, tender and quite good.

We couldn't pass up dessert—a slice of key lime pie was in order — and it was silky and tart with a nice, satisfying backbite. The Blue-bird, whose dining room overlooks the Leland River, has a large and well-conceived list of Michigan, California and imported wines by the glass and bottle.

# Blue Slipper Bistro

The Blue Slipper Bistro, 8058 1st St. on the corner, Onekama; 231-889-4045. Open Tues.-Sat. at 11:30 a.m.-9, Sun. at noon-10. Open daily after Memorial Day. Prices: Moderate. Rating ✦✦✦

It's Friday night at the Blue Slipper Bistro in Onekama, and the 100-year-old landmark is packed. Servers whiz by hoisting intriguing platters with breadsticks rising up like architectural pillars, and families and friends dive into big plates of pasta.

"We cleaned it up and now we're down to replacing floors and those kind of things," says chef/owner Brian Kissel, who turned this formerly funky biker bar into a Mediterranean-flavored eatery in early 1999. His menus change with the seasons.

Pastas are popular at the Blue Slipper, whose original ceiling beams, cedar paneling and oak bar are well preserved and lend a cozy ambience. Kissel offers a choice of many sauces—among them marinara, creamy tomato, roasted sweet pepper, toasted walnut and creamy artichoke. Diners can choose their favorite pasta and add meatballs, vegetables or Italian sausage.

Kissel, a Manistee native who attended the Northwestern Michigan College Culinary School, also turned the Blue Slipper into a nonsmoking restaurant, which is a sign he is serious about his food.

Indeed, check out some of the wonderful items coming out of his cramped kitchen: grilled duck breast with a portobello mushroom spring roll; veal scaloppine Conquistador with asparagus, crab meat and lobster sauce; chicken Gorgonzola; grilled lamb chops with bourbon pepper pan glaze; roast rack of pork with garlic mashed potatoes — and that's about a third of his large menu. Seafood, salads, sandwiches and ample appetizers round it out, and specials such as lightly fried lake perch hit the spot. Try the crème brulee with raspberry sauce for dessert—scrumptious.

Kissel worked for the Schelde chain five years as well as Marino's in Grand Rapids before he and his wife Cheryl, who runs the dining room, bought the Blue Slipper and started ripping out the old mirrors, big-screen TV and pool table.

The Kissels are hoping to expand the kitchen and add an outside deck, new bathrooms and do other building updates in the 90-seat eatery.

But right now, business is big, the crowds are flocking in, and the Kissels don't have time to do anything else but cook—to their patrons' delight.

# The Boathouse

The Boathouse,
14039 Peninsula Dr.
in Bowers Harbor,
Traverse City,
231-223-4030.
Hours:
Tues.-Thurs. 5-9 p.m.,
Fri.-Sat. 5-10 p.m.,
Sun. 4:30-8:30 p.m.
Longer hours in
season.
Moderate to expensive.
Rating ✦✦✦

Twice last summer I stopped by the Boathouse at Bowers Harbor on Old Mission, only to find a madhouse of hungry sailors and vacationers. Without a reservation, it would have been at least an hour before I could snare a table.

It's an entirely different story in the off-season. Only two other tables were occupied when we dropped by, so my husband and I pretty much had the place to ourselves, right by a huge wall of windows that framed the snowy harbor and bay. A fire was blazing inside the fieldstone fireplace, and under a pink and violet sunset, the view of Power Island was magnificent.

Sitting in what I've considered a summer place on a wintry evening felt exceptionally hip, like we'd happened in on a great little secret. The atmosphere in this casually elegant place with its comfortable rustic furniture, high planked white ceilings and nautical theme was gracious and unhurried, like life itself in the north that time of year.

We sat by the fire after we put in our order to take off the chill of the room. Our server offered to turn up the heat, but that seemed wasteful. Once we ate our first course, a thick, rich, smoky Southwest-style chowder with some Scoville-unit heat of its own, we warmed up considerably. I could have eaten a gallon of that soup, it was so delicious.

We also inhaled several slices of warm herb-crusted bread and sopped up a pool of fine extra virgin olive oil along with them. Next came a crisp Caesar salad with garlicky dressing, well-seasoned croutons and long shards of flavorful Asiago cheese.

By the time our entrees arrived, we were already nearly full, but plunged madly into a trio of sauteed crab cakes in a lemon-butter sauce and one of the $10 "Homestyle Sunday at the Boathouse" specials—pot roast with an herbed au jus, mashed potatoes and assorted vegetables.

Executive Chef Michael Bauer arranged our plates beautifully with French-style vegetables, caramelized onions and mashed sweet and Yukon potatoes swirled into a pretty mountain next to the entrees, which were first rate. The menu is full of interesting edibles, from shredded duck in wild rice pancakes to crawfish strudel and daily specials such as rack of lamb and blackened mahi mahi.

We ended the meal with a Lemon Cloud–a crisp phyllo bowl filled with lemon curd, raspberries and whipped cream. In season, blueberries top the dessert, which definitely would have been better. On the other hand, raspberries in winter are awfully good.

Our servers paced themselves well, clearing and setting without intrusion, allowing us intimacy and privacy, answering our questions about the menu, and when they didn't know the answer, they got it for us from the chef.

Between the great service, the gorgeous view, the marvelous meal and the decent price—our dinner cost $68 with tip, beverages and dessert—this restaurant's worth the drive, summer or winter.

# Bowers Harbor Inn

Bowers Harbor Inn,
13512 Peninsula Dr.,
Traverse City,
231-223-4222;
Hours: Sun.-Thurs., 5-
10 p.m., Fri.-Sat., 5-11
p.m. Memorial Day-
Labor Day. Abbrevi-
ated hours through the
cooler months.
Expensive.
Rating ✦✦✦✦

It's always fun to hear ghost stories around a campfire—one of those life-affirming up-north summer rituals. It's even more intriguing to hear ghost stories as a grown-up while dining out, especially when the spirit supposedly inhabits the restaurant.

Bowers Harbor Inn manager Tom Kowalski says he has turned off lights and blown out candles, walked away, gone back and they've been reignited. He has heard the heavy upstairs powder room door slam when no one has been there to push it shut. Others have heard the elevator go up and down without anyone in it, and have seen a figure of a woman with her hair in a tight bun standing beside them in a hall mirror.

It's just Genevive Stickney, the original owner of the circa-1886 inn, rattling around. Kowalski's used to her presence.

My husband and I didn't pick up any strange vibes when we were in for dinner. But perhaps because of Genevive, Bowers Harbor Inn is one of the most romantic restaurants we've been to in awhile, with its dark wooden floors and beamed ceilings, Pewabic tilework and ornate fireplaces, winding hallways and candlelit booths that are covered in white tablecloths and illuminated by handsome Tiffany lamps. We were seated at a window overlooking the lush front patio and the oaks, pines and water beyond, a magnificent view. We missed out on the spectacular sunsets Bowers Harbor is known for, but the dark, threatening sky made the experience all the more appealing. It was elegant but cozy, quiet but cool, with swing and '40s jazz playing softly and unobtrusively. Our service was wonderful, and executive chef Keil Moshier's cuisine was imaginative and prepared to perfection.

We started with a basket of warm, flaky rolls so buttery we didn't need to spread more. An appetizer of jumbo lump crab cakes arrived with crispy sweet-sour Asian vegetables that had been marinated in rice wine vinegar and sugar for 24 hours, and a pungent, spicy cilantro aioli for dipping. Next came a tasty salad of Bibb lettuce, crumbles of Gorgonzola cheese, sweet toasted pecans, dried cherries and red onion with well-made raspberry vinaigrette.

My husband's lamb chops were marinated in mint and Dijon mustard and cooked to his liking—medium well, yet still tender and juicy. I opted for another appetizer, a large and succulent scallop that was wrapped in bacon, pan-seared quickly and then finished in the oven. Both sat atop a crisscross of herbed potato gallette. Mine was accompanied by a sweet tomato relish. The lamb chops were finished with a mint demi-glace and accompanied by a tangy apple slaw.

Moshier, 34, a Kalamazoo native and New England Culinary Institute graduate, has been cheffing at Bowers Harbor since September of 2000, after stints at upscale eateries in New Orleans and the Grand Rapids area. His specialties range from Cajun and Creole to Italian, Asian and Southwestern. His plating shows the mark of an artist, with beautiful touches such as the delicate, fragrant bouquet of flowered thyme that decorated our crab cakes. It was fresh out of the large herb garden that grows in the back of the Bowery, the rustic, casual eatery (and former servant's quarters) that is attached to the inn. A full-time gardener, Eddie Ligon, tends the herbs and grounds of this 21-year-old Old Mission Peninsula restaurant, and she also offers carriage rides around the estate.

Bowers Harbor Inn also features a large and exceptional wine list, including bottles using grapes from its own vineyards on the estate—it won an award of excellence from *Wine Spectator* magazine in 2001. A meal at Bowers Harbor Inn is expensive. But mark my word, you will walk away with your spirits lifted—particularly if Genevive has her way.

# The Bowery

The Bowery,
13512 Peninsula Dr.,
Traverse City;
231-223-4333.
Prices range from $7-$16.
Summer hours:
4-10 p.m. Sun.-Thurs.,
4-11 p.m. Fri.-Sat.
Winter hours:
5-9 p.m. Sun.-Thurs.,
5-10 p.m. Fri.-Sat.
Inexpensive to moderate.
Rating ✦✦✦

My parents used to celebrate the coming of spring by piling my sisters and brothers into in the family station wagon after church and taking us to parts unknown. We ambled past open meadows and budding greenery with the windows rolled down so we could take in the sounds and smells of the new season, and we dreamed of warm summer days ahead.

That's exactly how I spent a late-March Sunday with my husband. We dropped by an early afternoon art opening at Hattie's in Suttons Bay. The sun was shining irresistibly, and as much as we both needed to go home and work, we instead drove for miles, up and down the winding country roads of Leelanau, back into Traverse along the glistening bay, then out onto the rolling vistas of Old Mission.

After several hours, we were starving. Handily, we were nearing the Bowery, the family-style eatery that is attached to Bowers Harbor Inn. We got there just as it was opening at 5 p.m., and we were seated by a roaring fire that warmed the still-chilly air inside the restaurant.

With its rough-hewn interior, high-beamed ceilings, vintage signs and cottage feel, the Bowery is the casual counterpart to the more formal Bowers Harbor Inn, and executive chef Keil Moshier presides over both kitchens. The Bowery was the servants' quarters and stable when the inn was built as a family residence for lumber baron J. W. Stickney and wife Genevive in the 1880s. Both restaurants sit on a 10-acre spread along Grand Traverse Bay owned by Howard Schelde and Robert Kowlewski that includes a vineyard, large herb and produce gardens and features dazzling sunsets. We managed to catch one on this lazy Sunday afternoon.

We ordered the grilled pork chops, which came with a mouthwatering fruit chutney, and the rich, ultra-tender, slow-cooked Yankee pot roast with carrots and celery. Both were served with roasted garlic mashed redskins (with diet-busting sour cream, cream cheese and heavy cream) and a just-baked basket of bread. We were in heaven.

I love the Bowery's plates, each ringed with bottles of beer—the restaurant features 50 beers from around the world on its list.

"We get a lot of requests to buy those," says chef Moshier of the plates, "but it takes so long to get them, we rarely sell them."

Besides beer, the restaurant specializes in fish, barbecued ribs, rotisserie chicken smoked over a hickory fire, steaks, and some interesting appetizers such as shrimp and herbs wrapped in phyllo and served with an orange-ginger dipping sauce, and spicy Santa Fe chicken and vegetable rolls with Creole remoulade.

The Bowery's windows overlook the Victory Garden, where Moshier and his crew harvest many of the fresh herbs and spices used each day in warmer months, along with peppers and a multitude of lettuces.

# Bubba's

Bubba's,
223 West Grandview
Parkway,
Traverse City;
231-995-0570.
Hours: 11 a.m.-9
p.m. Mon.-Sat.
Catering hotline:
231-932-9713. No bar.
Inexpensive.
Rating ✦✦

It's a tiny place with big food served up by a larger-than-life guy.

That would be Bubba, aka owner Mark Stehl, star of a campy local TV commercial that definitely fits the John Waters genre.

And that's what's so hip about Bubba's. When Stehl's manning the counter in the 14-seat eatery on Grandview Parkway across from the beach, the orders are flying, patrons are lining up for carry-outs and sit-downs, office workers are self-serving Styrofoam cups of soup, and to each and every customer, Stehl's slinging his wit. He's the man, in complete control amid chaos.

It's fun, friendly and a hot ticket at lunchtime, when folks crowd into the little diner, sharing tables with strangers, everyone commenting on how good their soup or sandwich or cookie tastes. Steely Dan, Ella Fitzgerald and Sarah Vaughn fill the air—not too loud to drown out conversation, just right for atmosphere.

"I try to keep it loose and friendly, light and familiar," says the 41-year-old Stehl, a native of Midland who summered at Skegemog Lake as a child and moved to the Traverse area after graduating from Michigan State University. He was studying to be a lawyer, but restaurants were his first love—he's worked in kitchens since he was 16. After years working for the Schelde chain, he opened Bubba's in February 2000, and the crowds have followed.

My friend Pam swears by Bubba's mahi taco, Stehl's northern Michigan take on the Baja Peninsula's fried-fish specialty. Stehl's is a low-fat update with grilled mahi, slaw and Great Lakes Salsa, a traditional salsa recipe with Granny Smith apples included for crunch. He also makes shrimp, steak, chicken, roast pork and chargrilled vegetable tacos. The restaurant also constructs large and small burritos with the same list of proteins, filled with seasoned tomato rice, black and pinto beans, cheddar and salsa.

Bubba's is deceivingly small. In the rear of the dining area, there's a large kitchen that turns out a feast of interesting appetizers, soups, salads and other specialties for the full-service catering business Stehl operates with his partner Jeff Wiltse, who owns Dish Café on Union off Front St.

My husband and I indulged in giant Bubba Burgers—seven ounces of fresh chargrilled ground beef on a crusty housemade bun. The burgers were topped with pieces of bacon, cheddar cheese, ruby-red roma tomatoes and shredded romaine and slathered in Bubba sauce —spicy mayo with ancho chile paste, Dijon mustard and other goodies. Before that, we scarfed down a couple of delicious soups, sold by the cup, bowl or quart—a fiery black bean and a meaty beef barley. We also drank some not-too-sweet fresh-squeezed lemonade, just as it should be made, and we were filled to the gills when we left.

Ah, but I will be back for more. The smoothies at Bubba's are superb—a banana-peach-raspberry is a good pick, and Bubba's doesn't use mixes or dairy, just fruit and limeade. There are big salads, big nachos and big sandwiches yet to try. And lots of big fun ahead. Bubba will make sure of that.

# Café Bliss

Café Bliss,
420 St. Josephs,
uptown Suttons Bay
(on M-22),
231-271-5000,
www.cafebliss.com.
Hours: Dinner from 5
p.m. Tues.-Sun. (closed
Mondays) mid-May to
mid-October. Catering
through the off-season.
Full bar. Moderate to
expensive.
*Rating* ✦✦✦

This lovely Victorian eatery looks like a cozy teahouse and serves a fresh, healthy menu of vegetarian and ethnic foods using organic and locally grown ingredients.

It's a friendly place, too, thanks to Benzonia native and former teacher Tim Johnson (TJ, as pals call him), his wife Ewa Einhorn and Tim's sister Sarah Jane Johnson. They're into low-fat cuisine, so you'll find lots of tasty seafood, soups and salads on the menu. Dive in to a savory artichoke canape on crostini or portobello mushrooms with sauteed spinach and toasted pecans, then perhaps some of TJ's cilantro and onion soup with fresh avocado and tomatoes. Or try the sea scallops with lobster Florentine over angel-hair pasta or char-grilled salmon with a maple-raspberry and roasted chipotle pepper glaze, all delish.

Life is too short to give up dessert, so make up for that healthy meal with a blueberry-peach crisp or a piece of chocolate-hazelnut cheesecake. Hey, you only go around once, right?

# Cajun Bayou

Janet Brownell has never been to New Orleans. She's never had formal training as a chef. But she opened a restaurant on Front Street with some of the meanest blackened chicken I've ever eaten.

"I just like hot food," the owner of the Cajun Bayou laughs.

So do I, although the chicken special, the hottest item on her menu, is definitely not for the faint-of-tongue. My husband gasped after a bite and downed copious amounts of water to quell the burn. Which was okay, because I had it all to myself, and it was fiery, tender and terrific, served with baby redskins, a huge helping of fresh steamed broccoli and quite a good deal for $10.95.

The shrimp Creole featured small, tender shrimp in a tangy, rich tomato sauce with pieces of peppers and onions over rice. We split a piece of pecan pie, sweet but not cloying, and it was quite good, but we found it was not made on premises. The next time, I'd like to sample the bread pudding with bourbon sauce, which is house made.

As the menu states: "Cajun is our name, Cajun is our game, authentic made from scratch," pecan pie notwithstanding. Entrees range from $7.95 for dirty rice with sausage and etoufee sauce to $17.95 for a sampler platter with bites of eight different entrees including shrimp etoufee, Creole and jambalaya, red beans with sausage and rice, dirty rice, chicken and shrimp gumbo and a mini Cajun roll. Entrees come with a house salad featuring good greens and warm

The Cajun Bayou,
810 E. Front St.,
Traverse City;
231-933-3300.
Hours:
2-9 p.m. Wed.-Thurs.,
2-10 p.m. Fri.-Sat.,
1-8 p.m. Sun.,
closed Mon.-Tues.
No bar.
Inexpensive.
Rating ✦✦

French bread. A spicy Green Goddess is the house dressing—a shade of green not found in nature, but tasty all the same. Other menu items include Louisiana blackened catfish and red snapper; chicken, shrimp or crawfish gumbo by the bowl or cup; appetizers of alligator, crawfish and peel-and-eat shrimp; and raw oysters on the half-shell.

Servers are friendly and wear straw hats. Cajun and Zydeco tunes fill the air. It's a pleasant spot with a nice view of the bay, something I never considered all these months of whizzing past the building. There's also ample parking in the back, a plus in this crowded part of town.

Brownell's artist husband Roger has airbrushed the walls of this casual eatery with Louisiana swamp scenes, and his framed art of sea creatures decorate the walls.

There's no bar here, but along with a full line of soft drinks they make some dandy Louisiana chicory coffee—they also serve the yummy, calorie-laden N'awlins fritters called beignets. Wash 'em down with that rich roast, and pretend you're on Bourbon Street.

# Chandler's

Just a floor below Petoskey's historic Symons General Store is Chandler's Restaurant, where diners wandering the Gaslight District can sit down for lunch or dinner inside the small brick-walled eatery or under the sun in the courtyard to sample some of the culinary delights that Symons sells.

Executive Chef Peter Hamm offers a lunch menu that includes fresh soups and salads, hummous, spinach and lobster ravioli, fancy sandwiches, burgers and quesadillas.

Chandler's,
215-1/2 Howard St.,
Petoskey,
231-347-2981.
Hours:
Lunch 11 a.m.-4 p.m.,
dinner 5-9 p.m. Sun.-
Thurs., dinner until 10
p.m. Fri.-Sat. Add an
extra hour in season.
Expensive.
Rating ✦✦✦

Dinners start with foie gras, risotto, Blue Point oysters or Maryland crab cakes and move into fresh greens, followed by grilled meats such as Black Angus beef filet with caramelized shallot jus and pancetta hash, provimi veal, rack of lamb, roasted duck or organic chicken.

# China Buffet King

China Buffet King,
1112 S. Garfield,
Traverse City;
231-933-9999;
open Mon.-Thurs., 11
a.m.-10:30 p.m., Fri.-Sat.
10:30 a.m.-11 p.m., Sun.
noon-10 p.m.
Inexpensive.
Rating ✦✦

A huge, well-priced menu, everything from cold noodles with sesame to dim sum for appetizers, 28 chef's specialties with many hot and spicy entrees, 30 different luncheon combos, priced slightly higher for dinner, and for folks on special diets, six dishes that are prepared without salt, sugar, corn starch or msg.

Jeff Cheng, a native of Taiwan who spent 12 years at TC's Panda North, is manager of China Buffet King, which has other outlets in Chicago, New York and Connecticut. This former pizza parlor was fully remodeled, in shades of mauve and with etched glass, flowers and new booths.

# City Kitchen

When I met Nancy Allen a year ago, she was in the early rehabbing phase of her new Traverse City restaurant and cooking school. The walls of the old house on Front Street were open two-by-fours, the floor's old underlayment was without a cover, and she was still looking at stoves and equipment.

But Allen, a certified culinary professional and former instructor at Peter Kump's New York Cooking School and the Natural Gourmet School of Cooking in Manhattan, exuded a certain kind of energy—that perpetual-motion, positive-charge charisma that the best culinary people possess. I had a feeling it would all come together the way she planned.

City Kitchen,
826 W. Front St.,
Traverse City;
231-932-2201.
No bar.
Hours: lunch daily from
11 a.m. - 3 p.m. Take-out
service and private and
catered lunches for
parties over 10.
Inexpensive.
Rating ✦✦✦

Her dream: A place where people from all walks of life could gather around communal tables, sampling exotic dishes from many lands and learning how to make them. The dream has come true. City Kitchen is thriving, and the cooking school's classes are filling up.

Indeed, during two recent lunches, diners were getting more than just sustenance. The big open dining room was buzzing with people eating spicy dishes like Hong Kong sesame noodles with tofu, striking up conversations with strangers sitting next to them, getting the lowdown on the goings-on in town. Other patrons were dining alone, lost in books or newspapers. City Kitchen has a coffeehouse feel with an ethnic bent, the right mix for a real city.

The menu features organic produce in season and year-round organic eggs and flour. City Kitchen's big board offers daily specials and a running list of housemade soups—I loved the creamy potato-leek—salads, sandwiches, wraps, noodles and quesadillas. City Kitchen just introduced a yummy pear, walnut and bleu cheese salad, one of my favorite combinations. Another not-to-miss dish is the tender satay with six plump shrimp on skewers and a hot and spicy Thai peanut sauce. Among wraps, try the roasted vegetable with chickpea and red pepper sauce.

Then let's talk about dessert: I can't go in there without grabbing a lemon square. It's beyond fresh, with a crunchy crust topped with creamy, zesty lemon and not the least bit low-calorie. Neither are the Black Magic brownies with Michigan cherries, the Breathless brownies with Guittard chocolate chips or the peanut butter chocolate pillows. Pair dessert with French-pressed Sumatran coffee and you'll feel quite urbane.

# City Park Grill

One of the many watering holes Ernest Hemingway haunted up north, this is where he was inspired to write his short story "Killers."

With its massive mirrored mahogany bar and tall ceilings, this restaurant has great eye appeal, and its menu includes spicy appetizers like grilled shrimp and Asian chicken skewers with wasabi cream and voodoo cocktail sauces and a goodly assortment of soups and salads. Entrees such as asparagus and wild mushroom lasagna with spinach and sun dried tomato cream sauce and whitefish with lemon, caper and basil sauce are a nice nod to the region's bounty.

City Park Grill,
432 East Lake St.,
Petoskey,
231-347-0101.
Lunch beginning at 11:30 a.m. Mon.-Sat. Dinner 4-9 p.m., Mon.-Thurs., 4 - 10 p.m., Fri.-Sat. Dinner menu only 10:30 a.m.-9 p.m. on Sun.
Moderate.
Rating ✦✦✦

Weekly specials, a happening Happy Hour and great live entertainment make this fun destination dining.

# Coho Café

Coho Café,
320 Main St.,
Frankfort,
231-352-6053.
Hours daily 11 a.m.-2
p.m. for lunch, 3-6 p.m.
happy hour, 5-10 p.m. for
dinner. Full bar.
Expensive.
Rating ✦✦✦

Most 22-year-olds have no idea what they want to be when they grow up—that goes for some 52-year-olds I know.

But Kim White started working at the Coho Café when she was 16, and the experience so thrilled her, she enrolled at the Western Culinary Institute in Portland, Oregon. Shortly after graduation, she came back home to Frankfort and bought the Coho Café from her mentor and culinary hero, Michelle Fierenehick.

Over winter, she and her family completely redid the eclectic interior, adding a more defined bar area, new seating, industrial-looking wall treatments and two shiny new restrooms (the old place only had one, and it was grody). They also redid the deck, which overlooks the Betsie River, with festive umbrella tables. It is a stunning view.

What was once a casually hip coffeehouse/café is now a white-tablecloth restaurant serving an upscale menu and drink specialties such as Blue Moon Martinis, Cosmopolitans and classic Margaritas.

Chef-owner White and co-chef Jeremy Whitcomb present ornately plated appetizers such as poached smoked salmon cakes with tomato-mango salsa, and black bean quesadillas, fresh salads, a small but goodly variety of entrees such as Asian-influenced baby back ribs, steaks, chops, pasta, chicken, fish and even a three-bean chili-stuffed sweet potato.

We dined at the cafe after it had been open only a few days and found a few glitches with the service, which White is tackling, and the summer rolls—deep-fried wonton rolls filled with julienned vegetables—were a bit oily. But the veggies were toothsome and well seasoned, the dipping sauce was worthy, and the slow-grilled baby back ribs were excellent—spiced with a mango glaze and smoky-sweet. They topped a tasty pile of chipotle-infused mashed potatoes.

Other dishes include pork chop and applesauce with sautéed apples and caramelized onions, five-spice chicken with stir-fried vegetables over jasmine rice, almond-crusted salmon, pan-seared whitefish, New York Strip steak with port wine butter and smoked salmon linguine.

The café also offers lunch with a to-go menu of fresh soups, salads, pasta dishes, vegetarian items and a wide range of sandwiches.

Judging from White's exuberance and youthful enthusiasm, I have great hopes for this happy spot along Frankfort's main drag. I'll check back after summer's in full swing.

# Creative Expressions

Creative Expressions Café and Deli, 4857 Main St., Onekama, 231- 889-4236. Open May 15 through October; call for catering in the off-season. Hours: Wed.-Mon. 10 a.m.-4 p.m. Closed Tues. Inexpensive. Rating ✦✦✦

Don Paone was making big bucks as director of training and development for a food-service company in Manhattan, living what was supposed to be the good life. But it wasn't. It was a living hell.

"I was caught up in the culture, status, working 90-hour weeks," says Paone. He was burned out—he needed to get out of Dodge fast. So he quit his job in the Big Apple, population 1.2 million, and moved to Onekama, population 515. Now, as the chef-proprietor of Creative Expressions Café and Deli, he is working the same amount of hours, but loving every minute.

So is the town of Onekama, whose summertime population swells with a large and sophisticated contingent of Chicagoans. Paone's inventive soups, salads, sandwiches, desserts, bagels and breads are wonderful, and certainly worth a drive if you don't happen to live in the picturesque resort town on Portage Lake.

Paone's credo: "If you don't have fresh food, you don't have food." The 41-year-old self-taught chef developed his appreciation for fine flavors while growing up in his Italian household in Newark, NJ.

"Food was the center of our life," he says. Paone experimented with recipes in his mother's kitchen and then on his own, finding success and learning from his flops.

He definitely has mastered the art. Consider this killer sandwich, the Quirky Turkey—a flavor combo that simply sings with smoked turkey, Havarti cheese, bacon, alfalfa sprouts and cranberry-orange mayonnaise on multigrain bread with sunflower seeds—his No. 1 seller. Or how about this luscious combo: prosciutto, fresh mozzarella, basil, sun-dried tomatoes and balsamic vinaigrette on housemade bread, which changes daily. Are you salivating yet?

In its eighth season, Creative Expressions has gone through changes "in a town that's not really a town," says Paone. In other words, tourist towns are great in the summer, but tough in the winter, when bills are due and the trade is sparse—a lament heard often from restaurateurs up north, so he and his wife Robin only do catering in the off-season.

Robin, 27, makes all of the desserts, and she has had plenty of experience—she started working in a bakery in Whitehall at the tender ago of 14. Try one of her tasty tortes, bar cookies or brownies.

# Crystal Club

Crystal Club,
9160-9166 Helena Rd.,
Alden,
231-331-6164.
Hours: Dinner, Mon.-
Sat. 5:30-9 p.m. in
season, abbreviated
hours off-season. Café
hours: 11-6 p.m. Closed
Sun. Main house,
moderate to expensive;
Café, inexpensive to
moderate.
Rating ✦✦✦✦

If you've wondered what would replace Alden's much-celebrated Spencer Creek, this is it, and it's wonderful. The circa-1918 cottage with the arresting view of Torch Lake, flanked by fragrant flower and herb gardens and deep-green pines, is now a compound of haute cuisine featuring a menu of small plates crafted by executive chef Michael Tuma and sous chefs Adam Bolt and Todd Tuma, Michael's brother.

The café next door features an array of well-priced wines and beer and an up-scale-deli menu of salads, soups, fresh breads and sandwiches such as grilled Havarti or flank steak, pan bagna and focaccia club. There's also a to-go menu of sandwiches, pastas and salads.

Michael Tuma hails from Mt. Pleasant, where he starred at Justine's and Café Edward after training under the late Hermann G. Rusch, founder of the first Culinary Apprenticeship Program in America at the Greenbrier Resort and Hotel in White Sulphur Springs, W. Va. His wife Ruth Tuma, a native of Midland, manages the front of the main house. Bolt worked for the Tumas in Midland and also spent time as pastry chef of Tapawingo in Ellsworth. And Jeff and Laura Cole—who originally owned Spencer Creek and opened the first Crystal Club down the road by the beach—are back, with Jeff serving as the wine whiz, among other things, and Laura running the front of the house at the café.

Try to snare a reservation at the main house at sunset – the pink, purple and gold display over Torch Lake is awesome. Soft classical music wafts through the rooms, the tables are dressed in fine linens, twinkling silver and pretty china, and the papered walls feature vintage prints and café market posters.

Start with a soup or small side salad of fine greens and a tart vinaigrette, then decide if you want to eat lightly or splurge. The list of small dishes changes with the seasons but might include fried calamari with Turkish gin sauce or goat cheese en croute with roasted peppers.

We indulged in three marvelous dishes—first, the crisp potato crusted salmon, which featured a moist, flavorful piece of fish atop sautéed leeks, surrounded by a velvety beet coulis, rich with butter, cream and demi-glace. Another dish, the buttery grilled baby lamb chop with a layered accompaniment of potato Dauphinoise, melted in our mouths, and the grilled quail with roasted carrots and pearl onions was tender and savory-sauced.

For dessert, just as the sun was setting, we tried the crème brulee—delicious—and the superb chocolate marquise, an airy log of egg yolks, whites and Callebaut bittersweet chocolate, heavier than a mousse, much lighter than fudge. When the weather's cooperating, guests can take coffee and dessert to the back deck and mellow out as the sun sets.

Crystal Club is a place for romantic interludes and fine wine and is not child-friendly. So book a babysitter, make a reservation, and enjoy the many fruits of this inspired kitchen.

# Dill's

Dill's Olde Towne
Saloon,
423 S. Union,
Traverse City,
947-7534. Hours: Mon.-
Sat. 11:30 a.m.-11 p.m.,
Sun. noon-11 p.m.
Inexpensive to moderate.
Rating ✦✦

The train isn't running around the room, the nostalgic photos are off the walls, the paper's gone from the tables, and the deep-fried pickles are just a memory. Gone, too, are the stage, the family band and the entertainment.

But Dill's Olde Towne Saloon, built by Bohemian Antoine Novotny in 1886 and one of Traverse City's oldest social establishments, is back after a major redo.

Those who remember the rustic interior with the Gay '90s theme will not recognize the place, which reopened Memorial Day weekend 2001. It has been polished, brightened up and transformed into a modern bastion of soft gold walls and dark satin-finished wood, with elegant pendant lights over the booths and handsome beams on the ceilings. About the only thing familiar about Dill's is the name.

But, as George Harrison sang, all things must pass. In the restaurant business, interiors usually get redone every five years or so. This was Dill's first since 1978. Barry Boone, owner of Boone's Prime Time in Suttons Bay, now owns the landmark, along with the cattle that the Dill burgers are made from — and they're big, juicy and char-grilled. Get onion rings with your burger. They're big, crisp, nicely flavored circles. Caesar salad with chargrilled chicken is a wonderful rendition of the classic, with lots of chewy shredded Parmesan, tender slices of chicken, thin red onions and crunchy croutons topping a huge bowl of romaine tossed with a tangy, full-bodied dressing. A couple of thick slices of fresh French bread make this a large and very complete meal.

The rest of Dill's menu is bar and grill fare – steak, barbecued pork, smoked turkey breast, egg salad and charbroiled chicken sandwiches, perch sandwiches and platters, subs, soups and salads for lunch, and an expanded dinner menu that includes steaks, chops, chicken, fish, seafood and pasta with housemade bread, choice of potato and salad or slaw. Desserts include pie, sundaes and baked apple dumpling. Service is friendly and fast.

On Sundays from 1-4 p.m., bar specials include Bloody Marys for $1.50, burgers for $2.95 and chicken dinners for $9.95.

Those seeking a quiet place to sup will not find it here, but Dill's was never that way. It's still loud, perhaps not as boisterous as the old place, but it's definitely a good-looking restaurant. And service is always first-rate.

# Dinghy's

Dinghy's Restaurant & Bar,
417 Main St.,
Frankfort;
231-352-4702.
Open for lunch and dinner Mon.-Thurs. 11 a.m.-midnight, Fri.-Sat. 11 a.m.-1:30 a.m., Sun. noon-midnight.
Inexpensive to moderate.
Rating ✦✦

If you have a major hankerin' for a Friday night all-you-can-eat fish fry, Dinghy's will fill up your tummy without depleting your wallet.

The 50-plus-year-old landmark in downtown Frankfort serves up a mean mess of perch or cod, cole slaw and choice of potato for the amazing price of $6.99. And the best part? It's delicious.

Sally Donaldson, the former owner and longtime chef, is back in the kitchen, making her regular customers happy once again. Donaldson and partner Carolyn VanCleave sold the restaurant a few years back to current owner Steve Christian. Donaldson stayed on as a part-time prep cook but didn't run the kitchen, much to the dismay of her intrepid fans.

"There was a gap," says one, "and it wasn't as good when she was gone."

After a long conversation with the new owner, Donaldson decided to take the kitchen back. When she sold her business, she was hoping to cut back on the 110 hours she worked every week. Right now, she's doing 40. When summer hits, she'll double the number, but that's still an improvement over her former workweek.

Obviously, Donaldson's culinary skills were appreciated on a recent Friday night. Dinghy's was hopping with diners ordering platter after platter of crisp fish and big racks of succulent house-smoked pork ribs, char-grilled and slathered with housemade barbecue sauce.

Another Dinghy's specialty are the tender sugar maple-smoked, char-grilled turkey legs, finished with barbecue sauce.

Dinghy's is a great place to hang out, what with its dining-car ambience, stained glass, walls lined with antique sailing memorabilia and old photos of Frankfort, and the car-ferry signs that hang above the dining area. It's loud and lively, the kind of local watering hole that seems immediately friendly and familiar—like the mythical TV Cheers, where everybody knows your name.

You have license to pig out on the fish fry, but my first plate, filled to capacity, was way more than I could consume. My perch was sweet, lightly breaded and very fresh, served with spicy seasoned fries, good coleslaw and a delicious hunk of French bread. My husband's cod was terrific, too. Those who want to splurge might consider the walleye special, a 10-ounce, pan-fried filet with slaw, French bread and potato for $11.95, an excellent deal. There are loads of other goodies on Dinghy's menu—soups such as creamy Southwestern chicken and twice-baked potato, Caesar tenderloin or spinach salad with warm bacon vinaigrette, pulled-pork barbecue sandwiches, hefty black angus burgers, big burritos, tempura shrimp, grilled steaks and a pound of Alaskan King crab legs with drawn butter for $19.95. You can't beat that price with a stick.

"This is not your low-cal kind of place," Donaldson warns. And that's just fine with me. Even on a diet, I can make some allowances for fat calories, as long as they are worth it.

So next time I'm in, I'm going to give those meaty-looking ribs a whirl—they smelled divine, and I've been dreaming about them ever since they whizzed past my nose on a tray.

# Elberta Beach Diner

Elberta Beach Diner,
735 Frankfort Ave.,
Elberta,
231-352-5273.
No bar.
Hours:
8 a.m.-3 p.m. Tues. -
Sun.,
closed Monday.
Inexpensive.

Edwin Carter never took formal cooking lessons, but as owner and head hashslinger of this Polish-themed nonsmoking breakfast and lunch eatery, he's watching his culinary star rising. Now into its third season, this 50-seat diner with the shiny white tile and green trim has been voted best new restaurant in Benzie County two years in a row by readers of *Northern Express Weekly*.

For good reason. His prices are small and his flavors are big — Greek, Polish, Irish and Mexican three-egg omelets; gyros; Polish pizzas with kielbasa, sauerkraut, cheese and onions on top; fresh-baked chocolate chip oatmeal raisin or maple-walnut cookies; irresistible cinnamon rolls; and Polish sampler plates with pierogis, sausages and stuffed cabbage. Yum!

The Detroit native and former Vietnam Marine is not Polish, but his wife, the former Doreen Jablonski of Hamtramck, is.

"I do better cooking than her," Carter jokes. But you'll find Doreen and their 14-year-old son Jason working at the diner on weekends, when Sunday crowds fill the place after church and the average wait can be 40 minutes.

But that's ok. Sip some of the premium-blend coffee and enjoy the scene. As Carter says, "Think of this as an extension of your house, or my house — I'm just cooking for you."

# The Fish

It opened two years ago where the former Blue Corn Grill stood and is about five miles out of Harbor Springs, off the beaten path, but if you're near Boyne Highlands or Nubs Nob, it's minutes away.

"The owners did a lot of research before opening, because it's in the middle of nowhere," says manager Cyndi Wright. The same folks who own Pearl's in Elk Rapids and the Red Mesa Grill in Boyne City decided on a seafood theme, and it's flown in fresh twice a week in winter, three times a week in the summer, from Foley's in Boston, among other high-end suppliers. That's why The Fish isn't cheap, but it's worth it.

The Fish,
5 miles north of Harbor Springs on State Rd.
(C-77) at Stutsmanville Rd.,
Harbor Springs,
231-526-3969.
Hours:
4-9 p.m. daily.
Expensive.
Rating ✦✦✦

It's upscale yet casual, a big room with walls painted appealing shades of blue and salmon, white papier-mache fish hanging from the high ceilings and a large piece of neon behind the bar that beams the image of a fish. It's loud and lively, and on the Saturday evening we were there, it was packed with parents with toddlers, seniors, singles and first-dates, and our server was quite pleasant and efficient until the very end.

Chef Scott Schornak, a graduate of Schoolcraft College's Culinary School and an alumnus of Tom's Oyster Bar and the Detroit Yacht Club, does the honors, and he delivers fresh, perfectly prepared treats from the sea. Everything is housemade at The Fish, from the sauces on down to desserts.

My table of four devoured a couple of superb appetizers—fluffy Maryland crab cakes along with shrimp tempura. They came with a wonderful remoulade and a divine relish that featured giant Peruvian lima beans and truffle oil. The shrimp also included a couple of battered, deep-fried green beans that were yummy—I wanted more.

Get here before 6:30 p.m. for the prix fixe dinner—soup, salad, choice of three entrees and dessert—for $19. After that, it's still a deal at $25. One of the choices is an excellent pan-roasted walleye, which two of my co-diners ordered and adored. And two of us got the grilled sea scallops, which were huge, lemony and luscious.

The New England clam chowder looked light and watery, but upon tasting, was robustly flavored with notes of smoked ham and bacon. Salad was a nice pile of good greens, well-mixed with a tangy charred-tomato vinaigrette. For dessert, we hoped to get the chocolate bread pudding, but they were out, so we got a trio of crème brulee – ginger, pumpkin, and an unusual chocolate anise—a good ending to a great meal.

# 45<sup>th</sup> Parallel Cafe

It's a fun, bustling, casual spot that serves up cool ambience and good food, done in bright hues of ocean blue and tangerine and filled with local artisans' paintings and artworks, all for sale. The waitstaff is cheery and the menu features interesting salad combos, soups, sandwiches, roll-ups, plus omelets, eggs, pancakes, waffles and a nice list of specialty coffees and drinks such as Sobe orange-carrot and Stewart's sodas.

45<sup>th</sup> Parallel Café,
102 S. Broadway,
Suttons Bay;
231-271-2233.
Hours:
8 a.m.-2 p.m. daily.
Inexpensive.
Rating ✦✦

Try the black bean hummous wrap appetizer—nice and spicy, a creative departure from the traditional chickpea version, and exceptionally fresh, not rubbery as is often the case. Or inhale a beautiful salad of fresh field greens with Asian chicken breast—marinated for three days in ginger, soy sauce and garlic—and Fontinella cheese with crimson tomatoes, toasted pinenuts and a well-balanced raspberry vinaigrette. Another tasty item is the portobello mushroom sandwich on whole wheat with sauteed onions, green peppers and provolone.

Indiana natives Tim and Bridgett Lambdin own the restaurant. He's a Ball State University and Purdue graduate with a degree in agronomy—turf grass management—who decided his passion was cooking. Breakfast is his favorite meal, and they serve it every day, all day, along with 20 flavors of fudge, the most popular being chocolate-walnut and Rocky Road, and a yummy menu of pies, cakes, cheesecakes and cinnamon rolls.

# Four-Forty West

Four-Forty West,
440 W. River St.,
Manistee,
231-723-7902.
Hours:
Lunch and dinner Mon.-
Thurs. 11 a.m.-9 p.m. ;
Fri.-Sat. until 10 p.m.,
Sun. 10-9.
Moderate.
Rating ✦✦

From the outdoor deck of this casual eatery that sits on the Manistee River, you can almost touch a three-story Great Lakes freighter or cruise ship as it floats past.

The food here is not as spectacular as the scenery, but diners will find a nice assortment of steaks, chops, chicken and seafood, pasta and a big salad bar that reminds you of a church potluck — you'll find great comfort in the Ambrosia, three-bean or pea and peanut salads. Sunday brunch features enough protein and carbs for a week. The wine offerings are fairly slim, but there's a full bar and a host of mixed drinks to keep you in a happy mood.

After you've finished, stroll Manistee's spectacular Riverwalk—it will take you all the way down to the swings at the beach.

# Funistrada

Funistrada, according to *The Oxford Companion to Food*, is an imaginary name the U.S. Army concocted to test soldiers' food preferences. Apparently enough GIs said they liked funistrada to make it rank higher than lima beans and eggplant on written surveys.

In Burdickville, Funistrada is a lively two-year-old restaurant serving Italian food and entertainment, as well as eggplant. And loosely translated, according to co-owner Holly Reay, Funistrada means "off the beaten path."

I stopped there one recent Friday evening for dinner with a couple of picky chefs.

Funistrada,
4566 Mac Farlane Rd.,
Maple City;
231-334-3900.
Open Wed.-Sun. from
5:30 p.m.; after July 4,
open daily except Mon.
Moderate.
Rating ✦✦

Funistrada's dining area is small and intimate, decorated in deep greens, mustard, brick red and, you guessed it, eggplant. With a smattering of tables and booths and a few tables outdoors, it seats 50 comfortably and could easily pass as a typical trattoria one might find in Roma. There's a small bar, comfortable seats and noise levels are at a minimum. All it needs is a strolling accordion player or guitarist strumming softly in the doorway.

The evening's menu is written on blackboards on either side of the room. Each night there are changing seafood specials, various pasta dishes and chicken and veal.

Our server seemed fairly knowledgeable, save for some of the vegetarian possibilities we inquired about. He was more than professional, however, and moved things along at a nice pace—not too hurried, just right.

He brought a nice, warm basket of fresh Italian bread and some house salads—a small antipasti plate with a slice of salami, pepperoncini, a kalamata olive or two and the greens, ribs of romaine. I would have appreciated Bibb or butter, and the dressing could have used oregano, basil or balsamic. We added some nice green olive oil, thoughtfully left on the table, which boosted the flavor just fine.

Our entrees were good: a large portion of lasagna, perfectly cooked roasted salmon and a heaping dish of lemon penne with fresh asparagus. The lasagna's hugely popular with Funistrada regulars, but for my tastes, it needed more punch and sweetness, al la Marcella Hazan. The salmon's sauce—puttanesca, the Italian word for prostitute—seemed too tame, even with the olives, anchovies and tomatoes; and the lemon pasta, with nice shreds of lemon zest, was underspiced as well. Garlic, please!

As long as I'm being critical here, the dishes were dotted with regular parsley, not the flat-leaf variety that punctuates authentic Italian cuisine. However, the parsley did liven up the visuals, and owner Tom Reay, a self-taught cook and St. Louis native who spent 12 years in the kitchen at Art's Tavern in Glen Arbor, obviously knows how to compose a beautiful dish.

Next time, I'd like to try the veal saltimbocca, which Reay says is the most popular item on the menu. Chicken can be substituted here, too, prepared with prosciutto ham and fontina cheese, topped with a portobello mushroom and finished with marsala. Other options are the portobello ravioli with acorn squash and cream sauce and the eggplant and roasted red pepper torte.

I heartily recommend the tiramisu dessert made by Holly Reay—a perfectly balanced blend of sweet mascarpone, espresso and brandy that sent us out of the restaurant with smiles on our faces. That said, Funistrada is fun, friendly, intimate, and I like it. It's not gutsy Italian, with flavors so bold, they're still dancing on your tongue the next morning, but it's thoughtfully prepared and a great little out-of-he-way spot for a sweet summer night.

# Galley Gourmet

I've eaten great salads and sandwiches in this sparkling Bay Harbor deli, and always walk away happy and full, wishing it were closer to Traverse. It's a Balducci's-style market with heaping baskets of Stone House Bread, high-end pasta sauces, jams, jellies, mustards, capers and the like, and there's a spot to sit on stools and nosh.

There are also wood-oven pizzas, calzones, Kobe beef burgers, grilled yellowfin tuna sandwiches, pasta and green salads, and a huge case full of fresh-made cakes and pastries. Sandwiches are huge and best to split. The chicken Caesar wrap is divine, as is the Cuban grilled pork loin in ciabatta bread with ancho chile mayo, red onion, lettuce and tomato. The market also features gift baskets, picnic baskets and an extensive wine list.

The Galley Gourmet,
4181 Main St.,
Bay Harbor,
231-439-2668.
Open 10-10 daily.
Inexpensive to moderate.
Rating ✦✦✦

# Good Harbor Grill

The Good Harbor Grill, 6584 Western Ave., Glen Arbor, 231-334-3555. No bar. Hours through Labor Day are 8 a.m.-9:30 p.m., gallery open 10 a.m.-5 p.m. After Labor Day, breakfast and lunch only from 8 a.m.-3 p.m., gallery open weekends. Inexpensive. Rating ✦✦

Before I ever moved up north, my friend and Detroit neighbor Janie kept telling me how I had to meet her friends Ann Derrick and Brendan Burrows.

"They own a cute little restaurant in Glen Arbor," Janie told me, "and they're really cool people - you'll love them."

It took me a year and a half, but I finally made it to their restaurant. Some friends of mine have a vacation place nearby, we wanted to meet for dinner, they loved the Good Harbor Grill, so there we went. It turned out to be a great evening with delicious food — I had a nice pesto dish and a fresh salad that came in a huge self-serve bowl for everyone at the table, and it hit the spot. The menu is semi-vegetarian, what Ann calls "utility eating — more like what people eat at home — keeping it simple," with salads, soups, sandwiches, whitefish dinners, stir-fries and pastas.

But the weirdest thing is that Ann spotted a furniture-making friend in her restaurant while we were there, and she asked him if he knew my husband, who also makes furniture. Her friend motioned over to our table, so right then and there my cover was blown, but that's okay because I'd already eaten anonymously and enjoyed every bite. Ann sat down with us and it felt like old home week, because we learned we have several friends in common. Before moving north in 1987, Ann and Brendan (natives of Royal Oak and Flint, respectively) lived on a sailboat for 10 years. Their two children, Cos, now 22, and Jason, 20, were born on the boat. They have worked at the Good Harbor Grill since their parents bought it and the Pine Cone ice cream shop next door 10 years ago. They haven't lost their love for the sea. Every year, they travel back to their beloved boat and hang out in the Caribbean all winter.

Ann calls her restaurant "a giant Odyssey of the Mind project"—with a team and coach figuring out how they're going to get a group of students together (the summer help) and serve 500 meals a day.

Though she says running a restaurant is a lot of hard work—"I didn't believe I could ever wash that many dishes"—she's up for the challenge of managing people, something she didn't know much about when she first entertained the fantasy of having her own restaurant.

"The hardest part is telling them what to do, to get work out of them. What's cool is when you finally figure it out and you have people actually wanting to work for you," she laughs.

Ann and Brendan opened a new gallery last season—with three trees growing out of the roof. Brendan, a former social worker who got his restaurant management experience at the Chart House in Hilton Head and St. Thomas, turned the deck that used to hold ice cream eaters into a gleaming, light-filled room that features antique botanical and nature prints, expertly framed by Ann. She has collected the prints since her days at Wayne State University, where she majored in anthropology and art history and worked at Detroit's DuMouchelle auction house. Foodies will appreciate her images of antique fruits, some that have disappeared from our tables, which retail for $20-$900.

I'll be back for a big turkey sandwich and a bowl of turkey soup with honest-to-goodness stock, both made fresh from the bird. They buy from local farmers whenever possible and they do not even own a fryer—hey, that's my kind of place. It's casual, homey, cedar inside and out, and my friend Janie was absolutely right—Ann and Brendan are very cool indeed.

# Gordie Howe's Tavern

Gordie Howe's Tavern & Eatery,
851 S. Garfield near Hastings, Traverse City;
231-929-4693.
Full bar. Hours are noon-9 p.m. Sun., 10-10 Mon.-Thurs., 10 a.m.-11 p.m. Fri.-Sat.
Moderate.
Rating ✦✦

I took some diehard Wings fans from downstate to this strip-mall eatery, and they loved the place. Even though there was only one server in the memorabilia-filled restaurant on a mid-Saturday afternoon, she cracked jokes, moved fast and made sure our table of four was well cared for.

I'd been here once before in a severe diet mode and enjoyed Colleen's Healthy Sampler—a delicious scoop of chicken salad with a nice flavor of dill, low-fat cottage cheese, cucumbers, juicy red tomatoes and carrots. So on this visit, I wanted to eat like the rest of the world – pizza.

It was everything I'd been lusting for over lo so many months of self-restraint: crispy crust, a sweet-spicy sauce, snappy mozzarella cheese, zippy pepperoni, toothsome mushrooms. It was superb. My friends, pizza snobs from Motown, agreed wholeheartedly.

What's more, the other items we sampled – perfect onion rings, a marvelous Marty's French dip in a crusty, high-quality roll with lean roast beef served with fries that tasted like real potatoes – were topnotch.

The rest of the menu is perfect pub grub: ample appetizers, soups, big salads and deli sandwiches that include corned beef on rye— "what we're known for," says the menu—portobello mushroom with Swiss and a smoked turkey club. There's the grill menu with a "Gordon Bleu"—chargrilled chicken breast on an onion roll with smoked ham, jack cheese and honey mustard—plus assorted burgers.

Entrees include barbecued pork ribs at $15 a full slab, all-you-can-eat fish and chips on Friday nights for $9, or a rib/hand-breaded shrimp combo for $14. Saturday nights feature roasted prime rib specials that range from $6 for a kid's cut to $17 for a king. The desserts looked promising—Sander's Hot Fudge Cream Puff, caramel apple crunch, Turtle cheesecake—but the pizza filled me up and I had to pass.

Gordie Howe is rarely at his restaurant, we're told, ever since he moved back downstate many months ago, but that's OK. We can look at all the fun photos of Mr. Hockey on the wall, watch sports on the many TVs around both large dining rooms, shop for team memorabilia in the gift shop, and maybe see a real Wing during summer, when the team moves to Traverse during its off-season.

# Green House Café

Green House Café,
115 E. Front St.,
Traverse City;
231-929-SOUP (7687).
Hours:
7 a.m.-3 p.m. Mon.-Fri.,
8 a.m.-3 p.m. Sat., and 8
a.m.-2 p.m. Sun. (break-
fast only).
Inexpensive.
Rating ✦✦

Many restaurant cooks have to labor in windowless kitchens, oblivious to any-thing but the food they're prepping. So you might say Wally Green has it made. "I'm thrilled to be able to cook and look out on Front Street, let alone have a win-dow," says the chef-proprietor of the Green House Café.

And we can watch him as he works, look-ing mellower than most.

Green took over the spot formerly oc-cupied by Joe Balsamo's, and I am happy to report the food is excellent. He serves breakfast and lunch daily, including eight from-scratch soups and a long and well-composed list of salads, sandwiches and burgers. Many of the menu items have a Floribbean twist, such as the citrus-marinated penne pasta tossed with baby spinach, dried cherries, walnuts, man-darin oranges and citrus chicken, as well as the soups.

"I love the Caribbean, that shows," says Green, a Traverse City native (St. Francis class of '67), who has worked in Colorado, Texas and Florida. Green also owned the Fife Lake Inn in Fife Lake, which he sold in '97. He never dreamed he'd be in downtown Traverse, let alone this location, which has seen several restaurants come and go.

"We looked at it over the years. I hadn't been in it since it was the original Stone Soup, and we decided, what's the only thing that's worked here? Stone Soup. So let's do that concept only let's kick it up a notch with eight soups a day and do the breakfast thing."

My lunch was a wonderful cup of chicken noodle with thick pasta, hearty broth, lots of vegetables and loads of flavor, along with a delicate rock shrimp salad sandwich on pita bread with light dressing, good tomatoes and lettuce. A small taste of potato salad seasoned with celery seed and caraway accompanies each sandwich. My husband had a Green House Dip — slivered, tender roast beef topped with Swiss cheese and portobello mushrooms on a toasted baguette.

Green's signature sandwich is the T.C. Reuben, lean corned beef topped with sauerkraut that is sautéed with dried cherries. I'm getting that next time. Or maybe I'll try the veggie sandwich with mixed greens, portobello mushrooms, tomato, artichokes, roasted red pepper and Havarti cheese on a warm baguette with balsamic vinaigrette.

# Grey Gables

Grey Gables,
308 Belvedere St.,
Charlevoix,
231-547-9261.
Dinner at 5 p.m. year-round.
Expensive.

Intimate and romantic, this antiques-filled Victorian inn is especially cozy when the fireplace blazes in the main dining room.

My friends who have dined here say start with the baked, sherry-infused five-onion soup or duck quesadilla, then go for a cherry spinach salad. The pan-roasted Norwegian salmon with grain mustard and balsamic glaze atop cherry couscous and crispy leeks is sublime, as are the steak and seafood specials. Grey Gables' wine list is superb.

This is high on my list for a visit.

# Hattie's

In the quaint downtown of Suttons Bay, the unassuming storefront offers little clue to the treasures inside. Hattie's—named after chef-owner Jim Milliman's grandmother, Hattie Fleming—is a lovely, modern restaurant done up in several shades of gray, with light-wood furnishings, soft music, low lights, paintings-for-sale by local artists, big windows that look out to the street, and a contemporary, eclectic menu.

Hattie's,
111 St. Josephs St.,
Suttons Bay
231-271-6222.
Open all year. Dinners start at 5:30 p.m., seven days a week.
Expensive.
Rating ✦✦✦

On any given day, Milliman and executive chef Patty Hickman offer an aromatic multicultural feast—dishes such as plump, Thai-style sea scallops; steamed shrimp-vegetable tamales; morel mushroom raviolis in a creamy sauce; California rolls with lobster and wasabi crème fraiche. The food at Hattie's is hands-down beautiful, on the plate as well as the palate.

The 20-table restaurant uses as many local ingredients as possible, including produce from Meadowlark Farms and Provemont Hydroponic Farms and wines from L. Mawby, Ciccone and Bel Lago, all in Leelanau County. Thus, diners shouldn't miss the luscious seasonal salad of juicy Michigan cherries, wild watercress, Gorgonzola cheese, toasted walnuts, and a light citrus vinaigrette – bitter, sweet and tangy. Or the restaurant's innovative recipe for whitefish, brushed with Dijon mustard, rolled in sesame seeds, pan-sautéed and served with citrus-ginger relish.

Room for dessert? How about a chocolate macadamia nut cake with chocolate gelato and malted chocolate sauce?

Hickman, 24, joined Milliman as executive chef three years ago, fresh out of Traverse City's Northwestern Michigan College Culinary School. She specializes in foods that are healthy and natural, and lives by her words: Keep it simple, fresh and delicious.

# Hermann's

Hermann's European Café,
214 N. Mitchell St.,
Cadillac,
231-775-9563
www.chefhermann.com.
Hours:
11 a.m.-9:30 p.m. Mon.-
Thurs.,
11 a.m.-10 p.m. Fri.-Sat.,
closed Sun.
Expensive.
Rating ✦✦✦✦

This market complex in downtown Cadillac features a deli, old world-style butcher shop and upscale restaurant. Austrian-born certified master pastry chef Hermann Suhs features nightly and seasonal feasts with themes such as Octoberfest, Michigan Game Buffet and the Austrian Christmas Buffet, along with sinfully rich desserts.

Hermann's all-made-from-scratch menu changes daily, but diners will find a wide selection of leafy salads, housemade soups such as French onion, Caribbean black bean and morel cream. Appetizers include escargot and German potato pancakes with sour cream. All sauces and dressings are made in house.

Fresh seafood specials are a hallmark of Hermann's, along with ethnic dishes that include everything from Japanese shrimp tempura to weiner or jaegar schnitzel. Steaks, rack of lamb, pasta and vegetarian dishes, roast duck and sauteed whitefish round out the menu, which features a large wine list, amazing desserts and an array of cheeses to finish your meal the way Europeans do.

# Hofbrau

The first time I walked into the Hofbrau's big cedar dining room and took in the scene, it struck me that it was a true neighborhood tavern, without the pretensions of the many moose-and-bear-themed tourist traps that scream UP NORTH.

There were students and families gathered around the tables, the TVs were tuned to sports but not blaring, the atmosphere was casual and convivial, the food was well prepared and priced, so what more could I want?

I wanted to return. And I did, and once again, it felt good.

Hofbrau,
2784 M-137,
Interlochen,
231-276-6979.
Hours: 11 a.m.-midnight
Sun.-Thur., 11 a.m.-2
a.m. Fri. and Sat.
Inexpensive to moderate.

Rating ✦✦

Former Detroit Piston Bill Laimbeer eats here when he's in town — last time he ordered the walleye, according to general manager Greg McAllister, who says he feeds most every celeb who comes to perform at Interlochen.

"We feed a lot of musicians here," he says.

Bruce Cockburn ordered a half-pound of hand-battered blue gill. Ian Anderson got the cashew chicken salad. Willie Nelson and crew consumed large amounts of perch.

The Hofbrau's history dates to 1928, when it was a general store that served liquor. After that it was Peterson's Tavern, and sometime in the '40s it was given the current name. Greg's brother Brian McAllister and wife Laurie Bowman have owned it since 1996, and remodeled all of the interiors in a rustic red cedar.

We had a short wait for a nonsmoking table on our second trip—the back of the house was full of nonsmokers; the front had several seats, so we decided to try our luck in the smoking section and managed to avoid sucking in any emissions.

Our service was fast and courteous, and our waiter came around to freshen our drinks several times while we dined. I ordered the half slab of char-grilled ribs for $12.95, and they were fall-off-the-bone tender, with a zippy housemade sauce and sides of coleslaw and cottage fries. My husband got the 8-ounce center-cut sirloin for $11.95, which was very lean, well-trimmed and flavorful, served with a couple of huge pieces of Hoffy toast—soggier than the Texas version with about twice the butter, so it stayed on his plate.

That's okay, because we wanted dessert, and it was a steal. For $5.95, four people can easily split an enormous six-layer piece of cappuccino cake and scoop of ice cream drizzled with caramel sauce.

The Hofbrau's chef Jeff Belanger offers an array of daily specials: Monday is $7.99 for an 18-ounce T-bone, Tuesday gives one-third off the menu prices and bottles of wine (the list numbers 100 bottles), Wednesday is Mexican foods, Thursday is a seafood extravaganza with 10-ounce rock lobster tails, oysters, crab legs and freshwater fish.

Greg McAllister says a line snakes out the door for Hofbrau's $9.95 Sunday brunch from 11 a.m.-2 p.m. Malted waffles, an omelet bar, eggs Benedict and Florentine along with dinner entrees such as beef stroganoff and prime rib are among dishes on the groaning table. The 112-seat restaurant is usually packed, and no reservations are taken. He says they go through about 300 chocolate-dipped strawberries, one of the brunch draws, each week.

# Kejara's Bridge

Each time I walk into Kejara's Bridge in Lake Leelanau, I feel like I'm having a flashback. Between the gold and eggplant Hippie décor, the semi-veg menu written in artsy script on the chalkboard and Joni Mitchell on the sound system, it could be Ann Arbor, 1968.

"People say that a lot, and neither of us have spent a lot of time in Ann Arbor until the last few years," says 28-year-old owner Sarah Landry, who shares the partnership with her sister Christen Landry.

Perhaps that's why the five-year-old restaurant is so successful. It attracts many generations, people who are looking to commune during breakfast or lunch, just like they did in college. There are big tables and small, mismatched plates, help-yourself flatware, napkins and condiments, a couple of sofas on which to relax and sip coffee, and plenty of reading material if you want to be alone. Every Saturday night they feature live music, either performances by Sarah and Christen or national folkie acts like Josh White Jr.

For breakfast, try the divine cinnamon-nutmeg-vanilla French toast made on mouthwatering Bay Bread, with toasted walnuts or almonds and local maple syrup. Or scrambled eggs with spinach, diced tomatoes, peppers, red onions, sprouts, fat-free ricotta cheese and smoked provolone. Fruit comes with each dish, and for $6 or $7, they're a deal. You can get a good falafel here—"in season"—meaning when there is more demand. They mix up batches of fresh hummus and boil their chickpeas instead of using canned. The marinated free-range chicken breast with pesto and provolone is dreamy, served with organic corn chips or pickle for $6.50, and the grilled smoked

Kejara's Bridge, 302 W. Main St., Lake Leelanau, 231-256-7720. Hours: Tues.-Fri. 7 a.m.-3 p.m., Sat. 7 a.m.-11 p.m., Sun. 7 a.m.-3 p.m. Closed Mon. Inexpensive. Rating ✦✦

turkey with Romescu sauce and smoked provolone is exceptional, too, for $6.25. Coffee is French-pressed and superb. Add a piece of coffee cake made with spelt and buckwheat and you've had a marvelous meal.

The Landry sisters graduated from Aquinas College in Grand Rapids. But they didn't study restaurant management or hospitality—they studied business, art and communications. In fact, neither had more than table-waiting experience when they opened Kejara's. But their partially organic menu, with produce supplied by nearby Meadowlark Farm, is a refreshingly healthy departure from the burgers and fries found in most lunch places around here.

"That was one of the reasons we wanted to start it, just because of the fact that there wasn't any place for us to eat and we really wanted to come home," says Sarah, who is a vegetarian. Both Leland natives, Sarah had been living in Ireland, Christen was just back from Colorado, and the building they're in came up for auction, so they decided to take the plunge and turn it into a community-based venue where they could express themselves. Their carpenter father, James Landry, fixed up the interior, with neat touches like the mosaics of broken porcelain dishes that adorn the pillars. City Kitchen chef/owner Nancy Allen helped them with the menu and showed them how to run the kitchen. They worked 90-hour weeks the first few years, but now the pace is thoroughly manageable, so much so that they can take days off—and the whole month of March—without worry.

"It's been quite the journey," Sarah says. "We've been really fortunate. We both really believe in something bigger than us out there, kind of pushing us along and guiding us in the right way, and that's really, honestly how this business started. It was just kind of following your heart and going through the doors once they opened and just trusting that whether you fail or whether you succeed, it's about the experience and the journey. It's kind of how we try and live our lives."

# Key to the County

I wasn't in a New York state of mind, as the old song goes. But when I stepped inside the Key to the County restaurant in Lake Leelanau, I was immediately transported there.

Certainly, there's no hint of the Big Apple from the outside; it looks like most of the little wooden buildings that dot the quaint village. But inside, the rich mahogany paneling, the 100-plus-year-old Belgian bar, the golden walls, the low lights and the casually elegant furnishings remind me of a tavern in Greenwich Village, where writers and politicians might congregate for a snootful of vintage port and a Cuban cigar.

Key to the County,
104 Main St.,
Lake Leelanau;
231-256-5397.
Hours:
Mon.-Thurs. 5-9 p.m.,
Sat.-Sun 5-10 p.m.
Expensive.
Rating ✦✦✦

It's a 135-seat spot that oozes with ambience and a history that dates to 1894. When new owners took over the former Powerhouse Bar from Elsie Lederle several years ago, they added a couple of rooms and refurbished another that features a fireplace to warm up in winter. Two private rooms can be closed off for intimate parties.

Lederle still drops by for a drink at the bar, which is a great place to sip a nice glass of California, French or local wine from a list of about 150 bottles. But the kickiest spot at the restaurant is its new French Provincial-furnished Viper Lounge, which boasts 16 different aromas of pure oxygen, accompanied by Orion Brain Machines with strobe goggles and ambience-sound headsets. It's $1 a minute for a nice, healthy buzz.

Key to the County is named for its central location in Lake Leelanau, and keys are part of the décor. They're the restaurant's signature, a welcome to the Key. Big, heavy antique brass keys are attached to napkin rings that are removed from the linens when the server takes your order, signaling the kitchen it's time to start cooking.

The menu features appetizers such as a jumbo scallop-chive crepe with shallot mascarpone and saffron beurre blanc, escargot and stout-battered frog legs. There are dinner Caesar salads with char-grilled shrimp, beef tenderloin or chicken for lighter appetites. We loved the Key's signature spiked shrimp ($22), rubbed with a paste of tequila, roasted jalapeno peppers and cilantro, served with a tangy black bean puree. It was perfectly grilled, and the flavors danced in our happy mouths. We also got the classic pile of perch, a batch of fresh, sweet, fish in somewhat heavy stout batter with caper tartar sauce. But the chargrilled tenderloin filet of beef ($24) with a tarragon port-reduction sauce was like buttah. And our desserts, a divine crème brulee and a richer-than-rich chocolate pate, sent us groaning all the way home. We spent a bundle, but it was well worth it.

Our service was well paced and highly polished, and the plating of each dish was a colorful, textural vision of impressionistic food-as-art.

The restaurant is the lovechild of Suttons Bay natives Gerald and Cathy Smith. Their son Troy, who worked under master French chef Guy Rouge at Restaurant Mirabelle in New York and obviously learned some amazing culinary tricks, is chef and general manager. James Bagi, who also worked under Rouge, is chef de cuisine.

There's entertainment on weekend evenings, which varies from jazz to rock and roll. Between the food, the oxygen and the music, it'll get you in a New York state of mind.

# Latitude

In its third season, this eclectic Bay Harbor eatery's well-seasoned captain is former Tapawingo chef de cuisine Richard Travis, who whips up enticing dishes such as Szechwan calamari or smoked whitefish tempura cakes with roasted tomatoes and herbed remoulade for the upscale types who visit the area.

But it's not just for the swells, notes the talented Travis. Though Latitude is sophisticated, it's casual, and there are enough choices on his ever-changing menu that diners can graze on brick-oven-baked flat-bread pizzas, eat lightly on a pasta dish or fill themselves up on elk medallions with wild rice risotto and cabernet cassis sauce.

Latitude Restaurant, 795 Front St., Bay Harbor, 231-439-2750. Hours: 11:30 a.m.-2:30 p.m. daily for lunch; 5-10 p.m. Mon.-Thurs. and 5-11 p.m. Fri.-Sun. for dinner; hours vary off-season. Reservations are recommended. Moderate to expensive. Rating ✦✦✦✦

Named after the 45th parallel that it sits on, Latitude is a hip, sassy spot with a great wine list and entertainment that looks out at Little Traverse Bay. In the winter months, Travis offers cooking classes. It's a culinary gem in Bay Harbor's Marina District, and I'm going back just as soon as I can break away from my computer.

# Leelanau Country Inn

The Leelanau Country Inn, 8 miles south of Leland on M-22 and Little Traverse Lake, 149 E. Harbor Hwy., Maple City; 231-228-5060. Dinner 5:30 p.m.-9 p.m. Wed.-Sat. (reservations suggested). Rooms $45-$65. Moderate to expensive. Rating ✦✦✦✦

It was a beautiful sunny Saturday afternoon, perfect for a winter drive through the rolling hills of Sleeping Bear National Lakeshore to our dining destination, the Leelanau Country Inn. It also marked a milestone birthday for my husband Joe.

We met the other couple that was joining us and checked into our rooms above the restaurant. Spotless, small and done up in cottage-chic, they were just what we would need. No phone, no TV, just comfy beds behind closed doors on which to crash after too much food and drink.

When our hostess seated us near the windows in the cozy circa-1895 dining room, we delighted that our menus were personalized with a birthday greeting for Joe.

Does it get much better than that? Yes. The wine list was long and afforded even non-drinkers a choice of dealcoholized versions. The L. Mawby Vineyards sparkling wine was dry and excellent. A piping-hot basket of rolls made with fresh herbs and lots of olive oil was so fabulous, we asked for another. Our salads were crisp and of high-quality greens, tossed with cherry-maple vinaigrette. The Swiss onion soup was rich, rich, rich—far more than I could consume, so I split it with my friend. On the other hand, the appetizer of two fluffy, lightly breaded Chesapeake Bay Blue crab cakes was so outrageously delicious, we ordered another plate. They are arguably some of the best crab cakes this side of Maryland, and that's coming from my husband, who grew up there.

By this time, we were loosening our belts, and our entrees were coming on a tray behind us. So we sucked in our guts and chowed away, wolfing down a couple of juicy Black Angus New York sirloin steaks in a mouthwatering marinade of black pepper, molasses, balsamic vinegar, garlic, olive oil and Dijon mustard that were utterly divine. We also tried a garlic-wine-anchovy-butter-sauced dish of scallops casino and a Béarnaise-sauced baked whitefish Neptune with crabmeat, both succulent.

Then the layer cake came out on a big platter with more birthday greetings and candles. It was a housemade carrot cake with not-too-sweet cream cheese frosting and tons of shredded carrots and nuts inside.

Service was exquisite. Prices were above average, but skip the appetizers and dessert, and you'll still have a great meal for a moderate amount. We lingered and laughed and celebrated my man's big 6-0. Then we waddled out of the dining room and up the stairs, continuing our good conversation in an intimate parlor across from our room. This is what people did 100 years ago for entertainment. It's a simple pleasure I highly recommend.

The chef-owner is John Sisson, a native of Grand Rapids who grew up in the Detroit area and graduated from Southfield High School in 1972. He and his wife Linda have written wonderful cookbooks, *Leelanau Country Inn Cookery* ($21.95) and its updated sequel, with some of the dishes I've described, and are bottling their own salad dressings and fruit sauces. All are available at the restaurant or on their website, www.leelanaucountryinn.com (where you'll also find discount coupons for dining), and at select specialty shops up north. The inn also features a lovely line of deep-blue, handmade pottery embossed with a handsome logo of the inn, priced from $5.50 to $22 per piece.

# The Left Bank Café

The Left Bank Café,
120 Park,
Traverse City,
231-929-9060.
Open for lunch and
dinner 11 a.m.-9 p.m.
Mon.-Sat., closed Sun.
Full bar.
Prices are moderate.
Rating ✦✦✦

It was opening night at the Left Bank Café, and the place was packed. Patti Steadman was not the least bit stressed, greeting the customers who streamed into the brand-new space as if they were guests in her home.

Chef Michael Steadman, Patti's husband, was in the kitchen, thrilled that he can finally cook without customers staring at him while he works.

The Steadmans just moved from the postage-stamp-sized, 14-seat eatery they ran on East Front Street for the last six years to a much-expanded, 100-seat restaurant and bar on Park. Any fears that the first night might be chaotic were immediately put to rest, at least where I sat, watching in amazement that everything was humming along and fully under control. No slips, no long wait, just great food in an attractively appointed, well-lit white-tablecloth setting.

We were seated at a table that looked into the main dining room and at the glowing fireplace, always a welcome touch in a northern Michigan restaurant. The Steadmans added handsome chin-level wooden half walls topped with ferns to give diners a feeling of privacy and to cut down on noise. Overhead, latticework features philodendrons. The walls are rubbed in shades of gold, and the chairs are Scandinavian-style and comfortable.

The Left Bank's wine list is small but adequate, with mid-range domestics and a few Australian and Italian bottles in the mix. There's an array of interesting starters such as Norwegian salmon puffs with seafood chowder sauce, peach waldorf salad with zucchini bread or smoked pheasant ravioli with portobello mushroom sauce. But we wanted something spicy, and the Louisiana barbecue shrimp with a crisp cake of arborio rice pilaf had a gutsy red sauce made with Sleeping Bear dark brown ale, herbs, garlic and hot peppers that would do any Cajun proud.

My salad, a crisp plate of tender hearts of romaine, was topped with the house dressing, a balsamic-herb, and the soup was a hearty vegetable that positively sang with earthy, full-bodied flavor and finished with Parmesan cheese.

Our entrees were fabulous. We were dying for seafood, and Left Bank had an ocean of it on the menu. I tried the shrimp fettuccine verde, a light-cream clam-tomato sauce with many shrimp over thick al dente noodles with a scoop of chevre in the center. The Boston scrod with plum tomatoes, wine, cream, mushrooms and capers was served on a bed of sauteed baby spinach. The fish was light and delicate, perfectly poached in a fine court bouillon, and the whole dish was rich and flavor-packed, yet not the least bit heavy. Other entrees included grilled medallions of beef with shiitake mushroom sauce, warm vegetable salad with chicken, roasted pork tenderloin with bacon, leek and tomatoes confit, roasted New Zealand rack of lamb and several other delicious items from Steadman, a Culinary Institute of America graduate.

We finished with a piece of tart key lime pie, one of many drool-inducing desserts that Patti makes daily. Her bread pudding with cherries, raisins, mandarin oranges and apples and the white chocolate macadamia nut mousse with raspberry sauce are not to be missed.

When my husband finished his meal, he was more excited than I've seen after any recent dinner. "This is a restaurant I want to come back to," was his enthusiastic pronouncement. Me, too.

# Lulu's Bistro

Lulu's Bistro,
213 N. Bridge St.,
Bellaire;
231-533-5252.
Hours:
Tues.-Sat., 11 a.m.-2:30
p.m. for lunch, 5-9 p.m.
for dinner. Sun. 4-8 p.m.
fondue dinner entrée
and dessert.
Expensive.
Rating ◆◆◆

The cold realization hit me earlier in the day that Paris would not be in the cards this year. *Malheureusement!*

Then I walked into Lulu's Bistro, and my spirits lifted. Greeted by a friendly scene in the swank and spare bar area, my group was ushered to a table in the back of the dining room, where we took in the high pressed-tin ceilings, artful pendant lights, minimalist decor and huge front windows. With its shiny maple floors, birch paneling with burnished-steel trim and soothing ochre and deep olive walls, the ultra-hip Lulu's easily might be found on a side street in the City of Light.

"Ambience is everything to me when you go out for a meal—whether you're out for a hotdog or fine dining," says Lulu's chef-proprietor Michael Peterson, who designed his sophisticated space from top to bottom.

Lulu's, which opened Dec. 12, 2001, is the lovechild of 32-year-old Peterson, who once cheffed at Le Grenadine in Paris and more recently at the magnificent Spencer Creek in Alden, which closed a few years back. It took him nearly two years to bring the dazzlingly understated Lulu's to fruition. He paid considerable attention to every detail, from the mosaic of broken mirror shards that he created behind the bar to the smart-looking Japanese candleholders on each table.

So on that frigid Sunday evening in Bellaire, with a table of convivial souls, we toasted a 33rd wedding anniversary, warmed up our tongues on a fine gratinee of French onion soup and pretended we were supping in the 6th Arrondissment on Saint-Germain.

Lulu's menu—casual French with Asian, Mediterranean and Cajun notes with a well-composed wine list — looked so appealing, it was tough to choose. From a list of appetizers like baked raclette with gherkins and Yukon gold potatoes or sauteed chicken and chorizo cakes with herb crème fraiche, we settled for meaty, house-smoked baby back ribs with a tangy ginger-hoisin glaze, and the Asian slaw that accompanied them was hot, sesame-scented and superb. The jumbo lump crab appetizer with sharp cheddar and sherry was not as spectacular, the cheese obscuring both the sherry and the crab. House salads were divine—field greens topped with flavorful slices of ruby-red roma tomatoes and a balsamic vinaigrette. A meal could be made of the greens tossed with bleu cheese, spicy walnuts and shaved pear in a tarragon-shallot vinaigrette for $6.

Our entrees were another difficult choice. My cavatappi (curlicue) pasta with garlic, spinach, bacon and shaved Parmesan arrived in an enormous bowl, twice as much as anyone needs, and was deliciously pungent and smoky. Other dishes I sampled were the hearty braised short ribs with Parmesan polenta and roasted root vegetable – sheer comfort food for a winter's night; and the braised lamb shank with garlic whipped potatoes and a painterly ragu of flageolet beans and herbs. The shank had great flavor but needed more time in the pan for the fall-off-the-bone tenderness found in Middle Eastern eateries. However, the grilled pork tenderloin, rubbed with cumin and herbs, melted in our mouths, as did the mahi mahi special – light, delicate and perfectly prepared. And our service was grand – unhurried yet well paced, although we were among just a handful of diners, so I can't predict how a crowd would go.

Like all fine meals consumed in Paris, dessert was in order, and we were in Nirvana with a hot fudge sundae with caramel sauce and toasted macadamia nuts presented in a towering flute, and a silky ginger-vanilla crème brulee with a nice golden crust. Cappuccino, latte and espresso are available, along with some inexpensive ports and dessert wines.

For the unwitting, Lulu's can be pricey—our tab for two with tip came to $90. Order an appetizer and salad and split a dessert or entrée and you'll walk away full with a few more dollars left in your wallet. Or go for lunch, when you'll find sandwiches like corned beef with Swiss and a Creole slaw for $7, a falafel wrap with feta, hummus, tomato and tahini for $6.50 or grilled cheddar with provolone on ciabatta bread for $5.

But my meal was worth it—and certainly cheaper than a trip to Paris.

# Mahogany's

Mahogany's Fine
Dining,
in the Charlevoix
Country Club,
9600 Clubhouse Dr.,
231-547-3555.
Lunch and dinner in
season 11 a.m. - 9 p.m.
Tues.-Thurs., 11 a.m.-10
p.m. Fri.-Sat., 5-9 p.m.
Sun. in season, abbreviated hours in winter.
Expensive.

Irish Chef Garrett Scanlan made Eaton Rapids a destination for Dusty's English Inn. Now he's thrilling Charlevoix palates with selections such as poached mussels champignon, potato-encrusted walleye, seared ahi tuna, steaks, chops and divine housemade desserts. This is on my list to visit this season.

# The Manitou

Fans say it has the inviting feel of an old lodge, with planked whitefish, trout, perch, steaks, chops and rack of lamb. It boasts casual fine dining on the southern edge of the Sleeping Bear Dunes National Seashore and features nightly specials, fine wine and imported beer.

This restaurant's high on my list for a visit this year, so stay tuned.

The Manitou,
M-22 between Empire
and Frankfort,
231-882-4761.
Hours are seasonal;
call ahead.
Moderate to expensive.

# Marina Ristorante

Marina Ristorante,
2404 Sunnyside Dr.,
Cadillac,
231-775-9322.
Hours: 4-9 p.m. Wed.-
Sun.
Closed Mon.-Tues.
Moderate.
Rating ✦✦✦

Something wonderful happened the last time I was in Cadillac. I discovered authentic Italian cuisine, the ultimate comfort food any time of year, any time of day—made the way I remember growing up in Detroit's *Downriviera*, Allen Park.

Little did I know that Loretta DeJulian Snider, who owns Marina Ristorante on Lake Cadillac, grew up nearby in the southwest Detroit neighborhood known as Little Italy, where I first learned the joys of good red sauce, homemade sausage and hand-rolled pasta cooked *al dente*.

When Loretta married Jack Snider some four decades ago and moved to Jack's native Cadillac, her family moved there, too. Loretta's parents Tillie and Rocky opened the restaurant soon after, using old family recipes, and Little Italy's northern outpost was born. It has been a family affair ever since.

Tillie's grandmother was the Countess of Milan. Rocky's family came from Rome, where his cousin still operates the family buffalo farm that supplies the city with mozzarella cheese. Other relatives were from Lake Como, and the restaurant celebrates their recipes and heritage.

Jack, Loretta, sister Joan DeJulian Linden, their children and grandchildren have operated the restaurant since Tillie and Rocky's passing – Tillie, a decade ago and Rocky, three years, but their spirits live on.

At Christmastime, Loretta makes what she calls Tillie's bread, or *pane*-Tillie—like *panettone*. Each family that comes in before the holiday gets a loaf of the sweet, fruity Christmas yeast bread.

"We've kept it up," Loretta says of the annual tradition, "because I love to do what she did."

She also makes the thin, melt-in-your-mouth crostoli pastries that some call Italian angel wings. But I'm getting way ahead of myself with those desserts.

The 215-seat, two-level restaurant has a lovely view of Lake Cadillac, even in the winter, when diners can watch ice fishermen and snowmobilers making tracks on the surface. The 85-seat upper level is used for private parties but it opens for regular patrons on New Year's Eve.

"Everything is cooked fresh," says Loretta. "In fact, most of the sauces are cooked once they're ordered—the Alfredo, pesto, puttanesca," she explains.

That's why we were so happy when we sat down for a feast that began with fresh-made rolls and well-dressed salad with garbanzo beans and minestrone soup and ended with housemade tiramisu. In between, our large group ordered well-prepared entrees such as perfectly tender and sweet veal marsala, luscious lemony veal picatta, a good spinach tortellini with cheese and meat sauce, fettuccini with garlic, butter and herbs, and a special of cheesy baked ziti with meat sauce.

Our Cadillac friends Joyce, David and daughter Sonya have been patrons for years and heartily recommend the lasagna. In the summer, they bike up to the next-door Tillie's party store for ice cream, and for parties, the huge selection of beers. Marina's menu includes everything from steaks and seafood to pasta, chicken and veal. Entrees range from $9 to $20. Don't miss the crostoli or housemade cannoli for dessert. If you know about Italian food, it's all made the way you remember.

# Mode's Bum Steer

Mode's Bum Steer,
125 E. State St.,
Traverse City,
231-947-9832.
Full bar.
Hours: 11 a.m.-2 a.m.
Mon.-Sat.
Closed Sun.
Moderate.
Rating ✦✦✦

My friends were incredulous. "What? You've never eaten at Mode's?"

They knew I was the consummate carnivore, a meat-eater extraordinaire.

But several years before I ever moved to the north, I walked into Mode's Bum Steer and quickly walked back out. It was summer, the place had no windows, and for my tourista dollar, only a light and airy restaurant with a view of the bay would do.

That was then. Now that I'm a year-rounder and outdoor grilling is testy in winter, Mode's definitely offers the panacea for my primal meat-lust. The stars here are charbroiled Black Angus steaks, and they're fabulous.

Mode's interior is cozy as a cocoon—dark and clubby, a classic chophouse done up in reds and plaids and natural oak. The tables are so closely spaced in the small, 70-seat main room, diners can ogle each other's plates and even take in their neighbors' conversations, which tend toward local politics and personalities.

"We tell people it's a cocktail lounge that sells food—no young kids after 5 p.m.," says Bob Mode, who with wife Anita has owned Traverse City's oldest licensed bar and restaurant (circa 1900) since 1975. "Licensed" is the operative word, he explains, noting that the 120-year-old Sleder's is T.C.'s oldest continuously operating tavern. Bob Mode does much of the cooking and selects all of the choice and prime Black Angus beef, which has aged for three weeks when he buys it and then ages two or three more weeks after that in his coolers to add more flavor and tenderness.

He says he goes through 800 to 1,000 steaks a week, including prime rib, T-bones, Delmonicos and center-cut filet mignon, Mode's most popular cut. Dinners are accompanied by a big baked potato, a slab of buttery Texas toast and a wedge of lettuce with housemade dressing such as thousand island or bleu cheese, both excellent. On weekends there's a well-appointed salad bar with mixed greens and condiments. The restaurant also serves fresh seafood, which accounts for about 40 percent of Mode's business, and meaty pork ribs. Mode says he buys the best food he can find and creates it from scratch in a very tiny kitchen, even his tartar and cocktail sauces.

"We're not the cheapest in town," says Mode, "but what I try to provide is consistent quality at a fair price. I buy the best beef I can buy, the best seafood and I do it year-round."

My party scarfed down some amazing steaks—the 12-ounce $16.95 Anita's cut New York strip was perfectly flame-broiled and more than ample, but for larger appetites, there's Bob's 16-ounce version for $2 more. Our foil-wrapped baked potatoes were big, delicious Idahos. Those seeking lighter fare can find items such as chicken cordon bleu or blackened chicken breast, broiled Atlantic salmon, Canadian walleye, shrimp, lobster or scallops. The lunch menu features an array of sandwiches – Polish sausage in a French roll, Canadian bacon sub, barbecued pork, burgers and salads.

Our service was expert, friendly and fun. Mode's is known for its low turnover – 80 percent of the staff has been working there more than 15 years, some for 23, others 18. There's much to be said about a restaurant with a happy staff. Between that and the sublime steaks, Mode's makes for some very merry meat-eating.

# The New York

The New York,
101 State St.,
Harbor Springs,
231-526-6285.
Dinner 5 p.m. daily.
Expensive.
Rating ✦✦✦✦

It's called New York, but it reminds me of Boston.

Hey, what's in a name, anyway?

Lots, actually, explains chef-owner Matt Bugera. His restaurant is named after the circa-1904 hotel that once occupied this elegant spot at State and Bay, owned by the Leahy brothers, who moved to Harbor Springs from New York. At one time the hotel boasted a bowling alley and an upper floor that was used for dancing and parties. Then it was a coffee shop until 1977, when the second floor was turned into condos and the main floor was christened the New York.

But it still looks like Boston to me, with its gilt-lettered sign out front, the massive windows that look out to the harbor and Little Traverse Bay, the dark mahogany bar and woodwork, and the ornate tin ceiling, which is the original.

For those weary of the formulaic meat-and-potato menus found in so many eateries up north, the food here is a breath of fresh air. Bugera, a Bloomfield Hills native who graduated from New York's Culinary Institute of America in 1983, calls his cuisine eclectic, classic and modern. Traditional dishes such as veal Oscar and oven-roasted Atlantic salmon share the menu with exotic duck and wild mushroom eggrolls and Shrimp Judy with spicy red Thai curry. The New York features steaks, lamb, chicken, duck, risotto and whitefish prepared many ways, along with sturgeon and pasta specials. The salads are excellent – try the baby spinach with bacon, red onion, mushrooms, pine nuts and cherry tomatoes in a red-onion vinaigrette.

I had a couple of amazing edibles on a recent visit. One, the Maryland-style crab cake and garlic-crumbed shrimp appetizer with a roasted red pepper aioli and crispy fried leeks. Another, tender rounds of roasted pork tenderloin with sauteed rice cakes, warm napa cabbage and a sweet and spicy sesame-soy sauce. Both were delicious and artistically arranged on each plate. Our server had all the right moves – professional, knowledgeable and there when we needed him.

The wine list at New York is impressive, too, though I would love some dealcoholized Ariels to round it out, and that goes for anyone's stock.

I'd been trying to get up to Harbor Springs for months. It seemed like a million miles away, particularly with the high-season traffic. When I finally made the trek, I was sorry I waited so long.

# NMC

Northwestern Michigan College's International Buffets are held November through April.
Meals are served in the Oleson Center, on the campus at 1701 E. Front St. Park in the Maple or Oak lot in the rear of the campus.
Call 231-995-1196 for more information.
Inexpensive.
Rating ✦✦✦

In my relentless pursuit of ethnic food up north, I have discovered an astounding oasis in the culinary arts department of Northwestern Michigan College.

"I think it's one of the best-kept secrets in Traverse," says Lucy House, NMC executive chef and certified culinary instructor, whose 15 students prepare international feasts every other week during winter semester.

"I tell the students, there's no place else around that you can eat true ethnic stuff. We're trying to change those culinary tastes up here – educate them a bit," says House, a graduate of Portland, Oregon's Western Culinary Institute and former chef of Crystal Downs Country Club in Benzie County.

The price can't be beat, either — $8.95 for lunch and $11.95 for dinner.

Consider the magnificent Asian buffet we savored recently: Sushi rolls wrapped in nori and served with a wasabe (Asian horseradish) dip so good and fiery, our eyes and noses watered. The Thai seafood soup was packed with shrimp, scallops, mussels in a fish broth. Toasted sesame scented the julienned papaya and carrot salad with roasted peanuts. Stir-fried bean sprouts, broccoli and straw mushrooms were punctuated by a rich hoisin-oyster sauce. Fried jasmine rice with fresh basil accompanied braised pork in coconut milk with a side of hot chili sauce. And skewered puffs of steamed, then grilled, golden chicken dumplings were paired with a garlic black bean sauce. Our beverage was Thai limeade made with fresh-squeezed limes. A bread basket with several types of sweet and savory Asian buns also filled out our meal.

After that, there was a fine array of desserts, including a luscious coconut-caramel flan, numerous cakes and architecturally designed pastries. It was quite a spread.

Before dinner, students assemble around the buffet's chafing dishes and recite the name of each item and its contents, just as they would do in a real restaurant. One student is assigned to each round table, which is topped with white linen and decorated with items pertaining to the dinner's theme. Brett Combs, a friendly 19-year-old from Saginaw, introduced himself when we were seated and answered questions about the meal as we dined.

"The public response to these buffets is tremendous," says House, "and it's a great experience for the students. It gives them hands-on experience in preparing something for the public, and it gives them deadlines and timeframes to work with. They do a lot of the menu planning, so it gives them the opportunity to find out what kinds of foods are going to work well for a buffet like this."

Guests are seated as they arrive at tables for six, so it's a fine way to meet new people.

"We don't have restaurant-type tables, so it does force you to interact with other people you don't know who are randomly seated together," says House.

Meals generally consist of an appetizer, soup, salad, two entrée choices, often a vegetarian choice, then side dishes – starch, vegetable, fresh-made breads. A bakery class provides fresh baked goods, plus all the desserts.

At the end of the meal, diners are asked to rate the student and the meal — in terms of presentation, greeting, attention, etc. Diners' comments become part of students' performance grade. We gave Brett all A's – it was a superb experience.

If you don't feel like cooking – or eating — at NMC, they will pack your meal up to go. "It's a good deal — a good value and very appealing to a lot of people. We usually have people waiting at the door to get in when we're ready to open," says House.

House notes that the college doesn't advertise these meals, but they have a mailing list and campus walk-ins, so the tables fill up fast. Get there early, or you might be turned away.

# North Peak

North Peak Brewing Co.,
400 W. Front St.,
Traverse City,
231-941-7325.
Summer hours: Lunch 11 a.m.-4 p.m. Mon.-Sat. Dinner Mon.-Thurs. 4-10 p.m., 4-11 p.m. Fri.-Sat. (limited menu until 1 a.m.). Dinner menu only noon-10 p.m. Sun.
Rating ✦✦

This loud and bustling eatery, which opened in 1997, features a gleaming brewery room visible from the high-tech bar are that produces about 1,800 kegs annually. Brewmaster Bruce Grossman offers five handcrafted beers and draft root beer, two specialty taps and English-style ale served at room temperature.

The restaurant's interior is industrial-chic, with exposed brickwork, shiny wooden floors, high ceilings, tall windows and walls painted in an artist's palette of lush shades. My favorite seating is in the booths, which offer some intimacy in the cavernous restaurant.

Former Bowers Harbor sous chef Richard Fetter is new this year at North Peak, bringing with him some new dishes such as sasparilla pork chops to a kitchen that turns out well-plated entrees, tooth-crisp vegetables and a good melding of flavors. Many of the recipes at North Peak incorporate the brewpub's products, such as the cherry porter barbecued ribs, the porter-marinated and grilled hanger steak, and the white cheddar and ale soup.

Wood-roasted chicken and wood-fired pizzas are among other specialties at North Peak, along with fresh fish and inventive sandwiches.

# Old Mission Tavern

It was one of those postcard-perfect evenings—velvet-blue sky, 72 degrees, a soft breeze off the bay—the kind of gorgeous weather that makes me stop and pinch myself to make sure it's all real.

I needed a scenic drive with the wind blowing through my hair. It had been ages since I'd been out to the Old Mission Tavern, so I grabbed my husband and our pal Richard and rambled the 14 miles or so along Center Rd., a lovely way to savor the sights and scents of the vineyards and orchards in full bloom.

Old Mission Tavern, 17015 Center Rd., Traverse City; 231-223-7280; open daily 11:30-3 p.m. and 5-8:30 p.m. daily. A good-size wine list. Moderate to expensive. Rating ✦✦✦

The sun filtered light through the trees. A couple of red-winged blackbirds chased a crow in mid-air. The fragrance of lilacs and cherry blossoms was intoxicating.

At Old Mission Tavern, diners get a bonus: a fine restaurant with a fine-art gallery, Bella Galleria, which sells original works from local artists and doubles as a banquet hall. Next door, there's another fine-art venue, owner and accomplished sculptor Verna Bartnick's studio gallery called Belle Arti, which showcases her art in a living-room setting. Outdoors, the lush gardens and lavish landscaping feel like a villa along Italy's Appian Way. On this particular evening, we were serenaded by the vibrant reds and yellows of a tulip garden in top form.

Inside the dining room of this rustic former garage, there are big windows to gaze out at the scenery and white-tablecloth service without the stuffiness of a formal restaurant. Our server was prompt, told us the specials, which included a pierogi platter that is served every Thursday night. A basket of freshly baked bread arrived still warm, and very fragrant.

There were so many delicious-sounding items on the menu, we had a difficult time deciding. We started with an appetizer of blue lump crab cakes in an exquisite sauce of white wine buerre blanc, but we could have had escargot, oysters Rockefeller, steamed shrimp, baked Brie or what the restaurant calls tapas Italiano – homemade pizza dough topped with fresh mozzarella, tomatoes, feta cheese, basil, garlic, parmesan and olive oil.

I was leaning toward the pan-seared medallions of beef with a gorgonzola, rosemary and pine-nut red wine sauce, but I opted for what I thought would be a lighter dish, the sauteed chicken with a mushroom and artichoke cream sauce. First, though, we enjoyed a well-composed salad of premium greens topped with marvelous bleu cheese dressing. Rich! My chicken was excellent, though not as light as I had hoped — two tender breast halves in a buttery sauce with cream, served with freshly grilled asparagus and colorful, nutty-sweet rice. Joe, my husband, dove into his pan-fried walleye in dried cherry compound butter, a very light and flavorful piece of fish served with the same asparagus and rice.

Richard wolfed down a meal of thin-sliced liver, sauteed with onions and tasty, thick-cut bacon, something that may not appeal to everyone, but he consumed it with fervent gusto. Every once in awhile he likes it, doesn't find it at most restaurants, feels it shows a certain amount of creativity from the chef when he sees it on a menu, and besides, he says, he feels better for having eaten it.

Traverse City native Ken Stoppa is the chef at Old Mission Tavern. He started there when he was 15 years old, went away after some years and worked for Bowers Harbor restaurant and the Schelde chain before returning to his alma mater, where he has put in another 11 years at the helm. His menu includes steaks, chops, Italian dishes, pasta, lots of fish and seafood along with fresh-made soups and salads. At lunch, Stoppa says the cherry-chicken salad with feta cheese, pecans and raspberry vinaigrette is the best-seller, along with the chicken Caesar salad.

It rained for a time while we were dining, but as we meandered back to Traverse City after a splurge of an ice-cream and caramel-topped brownie and key-lime pie, the now-pink sun was setting over the orchards and the sweet smell of grass filled the air. Life doesn't get much better than this.

# Pearl's

I take great pleasure in watching my friend Mike sweat. I don't mean that in a bad way, because he sweats when he eats food with the slightest hint of spicy heat, and he loves spicy food.

The first time I observed this, he was eating file gumbo with a certain amount of firepower. Beads of perspiration cascaded from his forehead, temples and upper lip. I thought he might be ill, because none of the other gumbo eaters had the same reaction. But that's how he gets his gastronomic kicks.

Pearl's New Orleans Kitchen,
617 Ames Street,
Elk Rapids,
231-264-0530.
Lunch and dinner served Mon.-Sat. 11-11, Sun. 11 a.m.-10 p.m.
Rating ✦✦✦

So watching him eat blackened alligator at Pearl's New Orleans Kitchen, the Cajun/Creole restaurant in Elk Rapids, was pure entertainment, like tuning into the *Saturday Night Live* skit with the guy who perspired like a fountain. Needless to say, the alligator was mighty zippy, just like Mikey likes it.

Judging from the crowds that fill this place even in the off-season, Pearl's has plenty of fans. Perhaps the only criticism I've heard about this restaurant is that people have to wait for a table on Saturday night.

"I don't think you want to eat at a restaurant if you don't have a wait on a Saturday night," says co-owner Fred Moore, who with partners Jim Cartwright and Mary Palmer, all Schelde Enterprises ex-pats, opened this energetic spot in May of 1998. They also own the Latin American Red Mesa Grill in Boyne City and The Fish in Harbor Springs. Palmer, former Schelde corporate chef, is a graduate of the Culinary Institute of America.

Step inside Pearl's, and there's a party going on, which fits its motto, "Let the good times roll." The room is all a-twinkle with tiny colored lights. Zydeco, jazz and blues fill your ears, and heaping platters of food, scented with the bold and sassy flavors of New Orleans, fill your nostrils.

In an area sadly lacking many ethnic treats, Pearl's comes through for all of us. Prices are moderate, the energy of the place is uplifting, and the edible options are plentiful.

Choose from an array of appetizers such as gumbo ya ya, oysters on the half shell, crawfish or red bean cakes or andouille sausage and cheddar grits. Salads such as grilled vegetable pasta or blackened salmon Caesar keep with the theme. Sandwiches include po' boys and muffuletta — round hero sandwiches topped with chopped olive salad.

How about one of the sides, like the sweet potato French fries? For $1.75, you can have red beans and rice, nice and hot, sauteed greens, Cajun dirty rice, corn bread stuffing and many others on a long, tempting list.

I inhaled Pearl's blackened pork loin with garlic mashed potatoes, and my husband ate a juicy char-grilled New York strip that was perfectly seasoned. It was tough choosing from the tasty-sounding dishes like shrimp Creole, spicy barbecued shrimp, pasta jambalaya, brisket of beef, or crawfish etouffee, which Moore says is Pearl's most popular item, but there will be other meals at Pearl's I'm certain.

We ordered the cherry pecan bread pudding for dessert, and it was my-tee-fine, indeed. I will get the flaming bananas foster or the hot fudge beignet sundae next time I have a few hundred extra calories I need to consume in an evening.

# Peninsula Grill

We were out on Old Mission, listening to jazz at Chateau Chantal one Thursday evening for the first time. The hot snap had broken a few hours before, the music was mellow and the fragrance that followed a much-needed rain filled the air with earthy aromas.

From the high ridge that Chantal is perched on, we felt a rush. The panoramic view from the patio of this winery and bed and breakfast inn—with its vineyards, rolling landscape and surrounding blue waters—looked for all the world like Tuscany or California.

The Peninsula Grill, 14091 Center Road, Old Mission 231-223-7200 Hours: Open 11:30 a.m.; dinner served until 10 a.m. Moderate. Rating ✦✦

As the sun set and a line of clouds were backlit like a string of pink and gray pearls, we wanted to linger in the moment—the marvel of discovery. So we headed for a restaurant we passed on the way to Chantal, and were delighted by yet another good find.

Brothers Mark and Jeff Davies opened the Peninsula Grill a year ago. Its previous incarnation was the Irish-American eatery, Molly's Bye Golly. Some time before that, it was Kelly's Roadhouse.

It's friendly, casual and outdoorsy inside, with rough-hewn wood, fish on the walls, two bars where locals gather, and two floors of dining. It's comfortable and easy, like we were feeling that night, and although there were a number of people seated at the downstairs bar, it was not so loud that conversation was difficult. Somehow, the acoustics work well.

Fresh pastas, steaks and good salads are the Peninsula Grill's signatures, as well as made-to-order pizzas and enormous calzones. Start with crab cakes or chicken kabobs, move into a cup of French onion soup or a baby spinach salad, then choose from grilled steaks, rotisserie chicken, a number of fish or pasta dishes, or try a sandwich, BLT or gyros.

The New York strip was tender, smoky and perfectly grilled, accompanied by redskin potatoes and crisp vegetables. It was a good deal at $15.95. I ordered the pasta Estivi, a giant portion of penne topped with artichoke hearts, ruby-colored tomatoes, asparagus and broccoli in a light garlic sauce. I could have used more garlic, but it was nevertheless a tasty, fresh dish worth the $11.95 we paid. We came with two friends for dinner, who got the NY strip and a huge, delicious half-pound Angus beef burger topped with Colby cheese on a crusty Kaiser roll ($6.95). Another couple who had been at Chantal joined us later for coffee and dessert, an enormous brownie topped with ice cream and caramel sauce that was divine.

We ended up closing the place, full of much food and good cheer, and when we stepped outside, under a full moon, a vibrant canopy of stars and a sweet symphony of crickets playing nearby, we hugged our friends goodbye and drove away, thinking: Man, we really love northern Michigan.

# Poppycock's

My husband and I dined here the night we decided to move to Traverse City. It was a lovely midsummer evening, perfect for strolling Front Street, and we wandered in and immediately felt a warm vibe.

Eclectic and urbane, Poppycock's is a place to find a good list of martinis or an imaginative plate of fresh pasta. Chef Paul Marek dabbles in ethnic fare, with lots of artichoke- and mushroom-punctuated specials, fresh fish, seafood and chicken, but Poppycock's is known as a refuge for vegetarians and nonsmokers—yes, you can breathe in here; the restaurant is 100 percent smoke-free. I love his black bean cakes with spicy corn salsa and the Middle Eastern appetizer plate with hummus and baba ghanoush.

Poppycock's,
128 E. Front St.,
Traverse City,
231-941-7632.
Lunch and dinner, Mon.-Thurs., 11 a.m.-10 p.m.; Fri.-Sat., 11 a.m.-10:30 p.m.; Sun. noon - 9 p.m.
Moderate.
Rating ✦✦✦

I also adore the divine desserts, another thing Poppycock's is known for, and even more so now that Martha McGinnis is doing the baking. She's also a busy personal chef with a host of clients.

"I really missed baking," she laughs, "so I went in and got the job."

McGinnis has added to Poppycock's repertoire of favorites that include huge Rice Crispie treats drizzled with ganache (bittersweet chocolate and cream), chocolate no-bake cookies, brownies and ginger snaps.

"Probably the most popular is the Chocolate Oblivion Torte, made of chocolate, butter and eggs," says McGinnis, an alumnus of the New York Culinary Institute and former chef de cuisine at the luxury Triple Creek Ranch resort in Montana. "It's a flourless torte, and then I frost it with chocolate whipped cream and then glaze it with chocolate ganache."

Salivating yet? I need a bite of chocolate...now.

# Punzel's

Out in the middle of nowhere—between Grawn and Buckley on County Road 633 —lies a Swedish cottage with cutout hearts on its shutters that is heavily guarded by Drekel, the troll.

Inside, there's Punzel—short for Rapunzel, the fairytale maiden with the long blonde hair—also known as Judy Hauser, a former model with long, flowing locks and Scandinavian good looks. As you enter her world, Punzel invites you to "experience the sight, touch, tastes, smell and sounds of our ancestors."

Punzel's,
8720 County Rd. 633,
Buckley,
231-263-7427.
Lunch served May-October;
call for reservations.
No credit cards.

Her rambling, five-room shop is filled with all things Scandinavian—from wonderful handmade Norwegian sweaters to a roomful of trolls. In between, there are handcrafted Christmas ornaments, children's toys, notecards, cookbooks, fairytales and Swedish and Finnish poetry. And, by reservation only, Punzel serves multicourse ethnic lunches, decorated to the hilt with edible flowers and herbs from her gardens.

"We have our own cheeses made for us in Minnesota," says Hauser, "and we age them ourselves."

One of her lunches might include an open-face Gouda sandwich, or a tomato-basil; pickled herring with wine and onions or dill, mustard and tomato sauce; gravlax marinated in dill and salt; fresh fruits and vegetables; fruit soup; chilled black currant, raspberry, blackberry or elderberry juice; and a homebaked dessert. An abbreviated lunch is $12, the full lunch is $15, and desserts are $4. She also sells the food items to take home, along with flatbreads, crackers and wonderful Swedish teas that are scented with sunflowers, herbs and flower petals.

It's definitely from another time, another place, and it's lovely.

# Red Mesa Grill

Red Mesa Grill,
117 Water St.,
Boyne City,
231-582-0049.
Hours:
11 a.m - 11 p.m. Mon.-
Sat.
11 a.m.-10 p.m. Sun.
Inexpensive to moderate.

This is another in a list of restaurants I've been meaning to get to because it has a good buzz, my friends say, and good Latin American-inspired food. Judging by Pearl's and The Fish, which are owned by the same folks, I think it's a safe bet.

The menu features faves like Cuban black bean cakes and shredded pork flautas; tortilla soup, Argentina steak salad, corn-roasted walleye, Brazilian skirt steak, Caribbean grouper, taco and burrito combos, tostadas and a large selection of margaritas and tequila. For dessert, there's key lime pie and chocolate quesadilla.

# Reflections

The only full-service Traverse City hotel with a free-standing convention facility, it is perched on the beach along Lake Michigan's glorious East Grand Traverse Bay, providing panoramic glimpses of Old Mission Peninsula, shimmering water and mesmerizing sunsets.

The full-service, fourth-floor restaurant recently received a People's Choice Award for Best Seafood from *Traverse* magazine. Chef Jerome Weisler prepares local whitefish with dried cherry tarragon butter and seafood specialties such as Cajun spiced blue lump crab cakes with Dijon crab velouté, grilled Atlantic salmon with dill sauce, and walleye with beurre blanc and brandied pecans.

Diners will find Alaskan King crab legs, Florentine chicken, maple pork tenderloin, rack of lamb, filet mignon and other tasty entrees, along with a good-size wine list; get there early and order before 6 p.m. and $6 will be taken off each entree.

Reflections Restaurant and Lounge at the Waterfront Inn Resort Hotel,
2061 US-31 North,
Traverse City,
231-938-1100
or 1-800-551-9283.
Hours: 5-9 daily;
Closed Sun. Labor Day-Memorial Day.
Expensive.
Rating ✦✦✦

# Rhonda's Wharfside

Rhonda's Wharfside Inn, 300 Main St., Frankfort; 231-352-5300.
Hours: 5 p.m.- 10 p.m. or so for the main dining room; the café below, which serves lighter fare such as salads and sandwiches, is open from 11 a.m.-10 p.m. and features indoor and patio dining.
Rating ✦✦✦

Ever hear of fried green beans? They're nothing like fried green tomatoes—i.e., breaded or batter-dipped and pan-fried.

They're stir-fried in sesame oil, tossed in sweet chili sauce, topped with crushed peanuts, and they're the top-selling appetizer at Rhonda's Wharfside Inn in Frankfort.
Apparently I'm not the only one lusting for spicier dishes in the north country.

I credit my pal Donna Moore at Rubini Gallery in Benzonia for tipping me off about the beans. She enthusiastically told me what I'll tell you: "You've gotta try them."

While you're at it, check out the rest of the menu at this casually elegant spot: it's superb. Start with a mixed organic greens salad with balsamic vinaigrette and aged Parmesan cheese, or a spinach-beet salad with ginger balsamic. You may want to order another appetizer off the menu, such as tuna sashimi, nine-spice finger ribs with Asian barbecue dipping sauce, or one of the day's specials. We loved the chicken spring rolls with an intense soy-lime dipping sauce.

If you want risotto, the creamy, labor-intensive rice dish that is Italian comfort food at its finest, it's a daily staple at Rhonda's, and each day is a different recipe. I loved the plump, pan-seared shrimp and scallops tossed with linguine, red onion, capers, sun-dried tomatoes, garlic and rosemary, though to my taste, the sauce needed a little amplification.

Rhonda Nugent is the chef-proprietress of this well-appointed, white tablecloth eatery, which she opened a couple of years ago. A graduate of Manistee High School and Olivet College, she earned her culinary degree in 1992 at San Francisco's California Culinary Academy, where the Asian influence took solid root in her cooking style. "It is one of my loves—I must have been Asian in a previous life," she laughs, adding that her intention is to share with diners a global menu that will surprise and delight—and it does.

The main dining room is spare and dominated by the massive windows that look at Betsie Bay. In the background, swing and standard tunes keep the ambience soft and palatable.

Nugent, who is a distant relative of rocker Ted, also studied art at the University of Kansas, then cheffed at Café Zoe, a pan-Asian restaurant in St. Louis. But Frankfort, where she summered with her family as she grew up, always held a special place in her heart, and we are lucky she decided to find her way back.

Next time, I want to try her oven-roasted chicken with a pear-marsala sauce. Or maybe the meaty grilled pork chop with spiced caramel sauce, or perhaps the Thai-marinated flank steak with cucumber salad. Now my mouth is watering.

Oh, I didn't leave last time without dessert, no siree. It was the most divine bread pudding I've eaten all year.

You've gotta try it.

# Riverside Café

The Riverside Café, 439 E. Front St., Traverse City, 231-932-0529. Hours: 11 a.m.-7 p.m. Mon.-Fri., 11 a.m.-3 p.m. Sat. closed Sun. No credit cards or alcohol. Inexpensive. Rating ✦✦

Sean Lorigan hums away in his teeny kitchen at the Riverside Café, white apron tied neatly behind his back, bacon sizzling, a few customers waiting for their lunches.

His new eatery on East Front Street now occupies the diminutive, 14-seat space that the popular Left Bank Café outgrew. It's a tough act to follow, but Lorigan, a 33-year-old with a broad smile and sunny personality, is up for the challenge. His lunchtime business is beginning to boom, and customers are coming in for early dinner or carryout, too.

Lorigan has put together a hearty menu of recipes that he borrowed from his late mother, Melda Lorigan. He worked at chains such as T.J. I. Friday's and Applebee's, as well as the Red Door Tavern in Columbus, Ohio, and GT's in Traverse City, and has assembled what might be called classic firehouse fare. The Riverside Café serves up big, meaty sandwiches, housemade soups, salads, and for dinners, an array of pastas, seafood dishes and entrees such as stuffed pork tenderloin and chicken breasts.

There are items for the vegetarian, too. Lorigan says his Veggie Nut sub, with seasoned almonds, walnuts, peanuts, carrots, celery, zucchini, Swiss and Provolone cheeses is his most popular lunch item, followed by the Davy Jones tuna and Swiss. He also offers a large fruit bowl with cottage cheese. Another popular sandwich is the southern Irish chicken breast with corned beef and Swiss. Sandwiches are served with a large helping of redskins, sauteed with Lorigan's special seasonings, which turn the spuds a deep golden shade. He won't reveal his spice mix, but the combination of flavors is quite tasty.

My dining partner and I ordered the bacon and three-cheese grilled sandwich—gut-expanding comfort food that I am partial to during heavy writing deadlines—and it hit the spot. We also tried the smothered breasts of chicken stuffed with crab, shrimp, mushrooms, cheese and ham and topped with more ham and three cheeses—a true fat-and-protein binge—but found the dish a bit bland for our tastes. On the other hand, Lorigan's Caesar salad with tender shrimp was marvelously garlicky and the romaine was crisp and fresh. While the chef's version—with black olives, tomatoes and hot peppers—thumbs its nose at the classic recipe, it was delicious, nonetheless. There are other intriguing menu items that I want to try next time I'm deadlining: The "Major Commitment" burger with bacon, ham, mushrooms, American and Swiss, and the steak and shrimp wrap. The roast beef on a sub bun sounds good, too.

The Riverside Café pours huge cups of well-roasted coffee, and the atmosphere is lively and personable thanks to Lorigan and his lone server, Derek Cruzen.

The prices are wonderful, too—sandwiches range from $3.75-$6.50, entrees are $6.95-$9.50, salads are $4.25-$6.25, soups are $2.25-$3.25. Lorigan closes at 7 p.m. but he invites customers to come in and get carryouts for dinner. Or dine in, then stroll off all that protein on the beautiful boardwalk that runs along the Boardman River.

# Riverside Inn

The Riverside Inn,
302 River St., Leland,
231-256-9971
or 1-888-257-0102.
Lunch and dinner.
Hours:
Memorial Day-Labor
Day, lunch 11:30 a.m.
dinner at 5 p.m.
Mon.-Sat.
Sunday brunch 10 a.m.-2
p.m. Extensive wine list.
Expensive.

It's quite a milestone for a restaurant to reach the ripe old age of 100, and this one's celebrating its century mark all season long.

Owned and operated by the Vilter family since 1997, who brought chef Tom Sawyer along with them, the inn is staging a number of special dinners, outdoor fishboils and wine dinners to do up the big one-oh-oh in style.

Sawyer began his cooking career at The Twisted Noodle, a modern Italian restaurant in Key West, Florida, then at Key Bosh, working under chefs Lisa Esposito and Monica Gotz. His menus at the Riverside Inn showcase local produce and combine his passion for Caribbean, Asian, and Southwestern cuisine. There are impressive items such as vegetarian tamales with black beans and roasted corn, topped with ancho chile, pumpkin sauce and served with grilled chayote squash. Or twin four-ounce medallions of grilled Black Angus beef tenderloin layered with grilled white onion, fresh tomatoes, and crostinis.

The newly remodeled kitchen now turns out lunch, dinner and catering. A cool cook's note: In February of 2000, after three summer seasons together, Kate Vilter and Tom Sawyer wed at the Riverside Inn.

Centennial celebrations in 2002 are Aug. 6, an outdoor fishboil; Sept. 14, a gala dinner under the stars; Sept. 27, Oct. 4 and Oct. 11, wine dinners.

# The Roadhouse

It's always a thrill to walk into a restaurant and like it off the bat. It doesn't happen enough. So often, mediocrity rules.

But that's not the case at the Roadhouse Mexican Bar and Grill in Benzonia. Freshness rules here.

The setting is wonderful, like a cozy cantina aglow with golden light from attractively rustic fixtures. There's a bar on one side and booths on the other that afford privacy and a certain intimacy. Service is friendly and upbeat.

The Roadhouse Mexican Bar & Grill, 1058 US 31, near the intersection of US-31 and state route M115, Benzonia, 231-882-9631. Summer hours: 7 a.m.-11 p.m. daily; abbreviated hours after the high season. Entertainment Thurs. and Sun. on the deck. Inexpensive to moderate. Rating ✦✦✦

New owner Gretchen Johnson, who took over from Jim Barnes last year, says freshness is foremost at the Roadhouse, and that's apparent from the moment the housemade tortilla chips and fiery salsa arrive with the server as you're greeted. Everything is made from scratch, from the Chilean potato empanadas to the deep-fried burritos known as chimichangas.

Johnson is no newcomer to the Up-North restaurant scene. Her parents owned Denny's Bakery & Restaurant, now the Riverside Inn, and she spent 12 years as a food and beverage manager at Crystal Mountain Resort. After a four-year foray into the vacation-rental business, the opportunity came up with the Roadhouse, and she jumped at it.

"We kept the same menu, and everything is made up fresh daily. Chips and salsa, our hand rolled and tied tamales, the potato empanadas, everything's just fresh," Johnson says of the 60-seat restaurant. She added an outdoor deck during the summer that doubled the capacity, and she says it has been a happy, busy experience ever since.

Quesadillas and fajitas are her top-selling items. "I don't think it's authentic Mexican, but it's real close," she says. Her main cook, "chef Miguel," as he likes to be called, is a 21-year-old from Mexico. He and the other cooks, Derrick and Barb, prepare the daily feast.

We dove into a couple of enormous platters after pigging out on the salsa, which was so delicious, I poured the last drizzle onto my spoon and slurped it up—good to the very last drop. My enchiladas were a combo, two with cheese and one with shredded chicken. Both were nice and spicy with sides of well-seasoned rice and black beans, something I enjoy far more than the mushy refried stuff (Roadhouse has refried, too, but not mushy). My husband got the quesadilla filled with Tequila-marinated steak, cheese, onions and tomatoes, and it was excellent, tender and accompanied by a sensational smoked-tomato salsa.

The menu offers a number of combo plates, lighter fare such as salads or a salsa sampler, wraps served with black bean corn relish, and a la carte items such as tacos, tamales, burritos and guacamole. The Roadhouse also boasts a large Margarita bar and specialty cocktails such as the Mexican Lollipop.

Breakfast and lunch are new this year. Breakfast offerings include burritos, fritattas, huevos rancheros and quesadillas. Lunch is a scaled-down version of the dinner menu, along with jalapeno cheddar burgers and wraps.

Prices are great, too. The two of us waddled away from the Roadhouse that night for a mere $25, with tip, and an evening of great-sounding entertainment. I'd say this is a place that will be worth the drive all year long.

# Rose Room

Ernest Hemingway and syndicated sex-ologist Dr. Ruth Westheimer slept at the Perry Hotel, as did Bob Hope, Art Linkletter, Mickey Rooney and the cast and crew of MTV's "Real World."

Presumably some of those celebs ate in the H.O. Rose Room, too. And so did I.

It's downtown Petoskey's only hotel, a circa-1899 gem in the city's historic Gaslight District with a wraparound, wicker-clad front porch and killer views of Lake Michigan's Little Traverse Bay.

The white-tablecloth, silver- and china-clad Rose Room might look formal, and you can certainly dress up, but like most

The H. O. Rose Room, Stafford's Perry Hotel, Bay and Lewis Streets in downtown Petoskey's Gaslight District, 800-737-1899. Open for breakfast, lunch and dinner. Moderate to expensive Rating ✦✦✦

of northern Michigan, casual clothes are fine. The room features a panoramic view of the bay along with breakfast, lunch and dinner, accompanied by piano on the weekends. The wine list is extensive and the menu is well-prepared American—steaks and chops, seafood, fresh fish, pasta and salads, divine desserts—with a regional twist, such as eggs scrambled with morel mushrooms or cherry French toast for breakfast; whitefish sandwich with remoulade for lunch; or Michigan perch sautéed in sherry-garlic butter for dinner. The Sunday champagne brunch buffet is a royal feast, often accompanied by a saxophonist, and service is extraordinary—positively civil.

The recently expanded Noggin Room in the hotel's lower level is North Woods casual and offers light jazz and folk from local entertainers, a "Hall of Foam" list of 50 specialty beers, imports and microbrews, and a menu of sandwiches, salads, pizza and other light bites. In warm months, the stunning Rose Garden Veranda seats 50 for al fresco dining, with a heated conservatory roof that tackles any chill from the bay, and opulent perennial beds that are tended by a full-time gardener.

# The Rowe

The Rowe,
6303 Lake St.,
Ellsworth,
(toll-free) 866-432-5873
or 231-588-7351.
Open at 6 p.m. seven
days a week, year-
round.
Expensive.
Rating ✦✦✦

Open since 1972, it's the pride of northern Michigan's regional-food pioneer, Wes Westhoven. The rustic 1947 cottage's kitchen features French country cuisine by home-grown executive chef Todd Veenstra, a graduate of Grand Rapids Community College's culinary arts program.

The Rowe's kitchen spawned the legendary chef-owners of Tapawingo and Hattie's, Pete Peterson and Jim Milliman, respectively, and under Veenstra's hand produces dishes such as pork tenderloin with orange bourbon, duck Magret with pears and green peppercorns, Chilean sea bass Provençal and veal tenderloin with wild mushroom port.

It has a loyal following, and the restaurant boasts one of the largest cellars in Michigan, with many rare and old vintages. The Saturday wine lunches are paired with French cheeses, sausages and fruits.

# Sagamore's

Perched on a mile-long beach of sugar sand, the nouveau-Victorian Inn at Bay Harbor looks out at a stretch of Lake Michigan known as Little Traverse Bay that could give the Emerald Gulf Coast a run for its money any day.

Lunch or dinner in the 124-seat fine-dining room at Sagamore's is lovely, surrounded by the warmth of elegant red walls and vintage prints, the tables set with Villeroy and Boch tableware, and such a stunning view. I nibbled alone one afternoon on a light meal of Asian-inspired spring rolls and chicken wraps delivered by a most solicitous server, gazed out at the turquoise water and paged through a novel, feeling evermore serene.

Sagamore's at The Inn at Bay Harbor,
3600 Village Harbor Dr.,
Bay Harbor,
231-439-4059,
800-GO-BOYNE,
www.innatbayharbor.com.
Hours:
Breakfast 8-10a.m.,
lunch 11:30 a.m.-2:30 p.m.,
dinner 6-10 p.m.
Extensive wine list.
Moderate to expensive.
Rating ✦✦✦✦

For dinner, I ordered room service—more appetizers from a menu of delicious-sounding dishes assembled by executive chef and Culinary Institute of America graduate Chris Andersen. The tricolored herbed shrimp with basil and red pepper sauces with slow-roasted caramelized beans and a baby spinach salad with warm bacon vinaigrette were sublime. After dinner, I tossed rose petals into my Jacuzzi and lingered under the jets. Then I slipped under the goose-down covers and watched the sun set. Life doesn't get much better than this.

# Sleder's

Sleder's Family Tavern, 717 Randolph Street, Traverse City; 231-947-9213. Hours: Mon.-Thurs. 11-11, Fri.-Sat. 11 a.m.-midnight, Sun. noon-9 p.m.
Rating ✦✦

Whenever my downstate pals Bob and Jacqueline spend time up north, they make a pilgrimage to Sleder's Family Tavern on Randolph Street. At nearly 120 years, it's one of the oldest continuously operating taverns in the state, a place where people congregate to celebrate history, knock down some brewskis, eat a burger with fries, and when they're good and loose, kiss the moose on the wall.

I scarfed down an olive burger with owner Deb Cairns the other day, who turned me on to the rich history of Sleder's, which she and husband Brian Cairns purchased in 1992. They loved the tavern so much, they held their wedding reception on the porch the weekend before they officially reopened. Traverse City native Deb grew up at the top of nearby Wayne Hill, "when the view wasn't such a big deal and the walk was," and always had a soft spot for Sleder's, built by Bohemian wheelwright Vencel Sleder and pals, who crafted it from wooden slabs from the local sawmills.

When Deb and Brian took over the landmark, they wanted to keep it exactly how it has been for all these years, right down to the original tin ceiling, wooden booths, round oak tables and ice cream parlor chairs.

"The front and back bar are all original," says Deb. "They've had a little work—to repair wood rot—and there are worry holes across the top of the bar," places where patrons find low spots and rub them ever lower while they're bellied up. All kinds of animal mounts hang along the walls, as do historic Traverse City scenes, signs and other memorabilia—enough to keep your eyes wandering all evening long and a grand source for local lore.

Burgers are the number one item sold at Sleder's—the ground chuck variety first and the buffalo second. Deb's dad, Earl Jodway, cut meat for Oleson's for 43 years, so that's where the meat comes from. Deb estimates she sells about 160 Sleder burgers on a good day and slices about 360 potatoes nightly for the hand-cut French fries.

There are many other items on Sleder's menu: marinated chicken wings served with spicy hot sauce, deep-fried pickle spears (if you miss the ones Dill's used to serve, they're here), all manner of salads, homemade soups, fish and chips, cod, perch, walleye, whitefish, shrimp and smelt dinners, oven-roasted baby back ribs, barbecued chicken and steaks.

As for that moose—which must be kissed if you want to say you've really been to Sleder's—it's named Randolph. It replaced the massive moose old-timers once sidled up a stepladder to smack.

"The original moose is here, but the lips are falling off," laughs Deb, who bought the younger mount from a hunter in Minnesota. Patrons named it Randolph in a contest in the summer of '94.

So here's the deal: When you hear a bell ring, Randolph has been smooched by yet another soul. It's a Traverse tradition.

# Stafford's Bay View Inn

Stafford's Bay View Inn, 2011 Woodland Ave. off US-31 North, Petoskey, 231-347-2771, 800-258-1886 or www.staffords.com. Breakfast, lunch and dinner June 14 - Sept. 8. Varying hours in winter. Call for reservations and information. Moderate to expensive. Rating ✦✦✦

Gracious and elegant, the 1886 inn's wraparound porch and red-checked dining rooms look out at Little Traverse Bay. Sunday brunch is enormous and opulent. after you eat, you can stroll the glorious gardens of the historic Bay View Association. Try a tender pork chop, marinated in apple cider, or the cherry-pepper steak served with a port demiglace laced with dried tart cherries. No alcohol.

# Tapawingo

I always hold Tapawingo in the highest esteem, for its innovative flavors, level of service and attention to detail, and wasn't disappointed when I sampled some dishes made by a cooking class at the Ellsworth icon recently.

It was an amazingly warm spring afternoon. We dined on the patio, staring at the powder-blue sky and the graceful swans on St. Clair Lake, savoring the exotic tastes and textures of chick pea soup topped with cumin-infused harissa, radish and croutons; olive oil-poached snapper and artichokes barigoule atop citrus-scented Israeli couscous; mussels mariniere; rustic ciabatta and flat piadini bread, the latter specked with pungent kalamata olives. For dessert, a molded molten chocolate cake with a warm chocolate center was served with banana ice cream and chocolate and tangerine sauces.

> Tapawingo,
> 9502 Lake St.,
> Ellsworth,
> 231-588-7971
> or www.tapawingo.net.
> Patio dining is 5:30-9 p.m.
> Tues.-Sun. (weather
> permitting).
> The dining room is open
> daily in the high season
> from 5:30 p.m.-9:30 p.m.
> Reservations are required.
> Very expensive.
> Rating ✦✦✦✦✦

The hands-on class, "Cooking and Dining in the Style of Tapawingo"—modern American cuisine with a fresh twist—lasted two days and included five meals and wine for $375. Chef/owner Pete Peterson and executive chef Stuart Brioza, formerly of Saverin in Chicago, and pastry chef Nicole Krasinski offer one- and two-day classes several times a year, and judging from the meal I experienced, it's well worth the expense.

I also treated myself to Tapawingo's annual herb luncheon in June, each part of the wonderful meal incorporating a fresh herb or two with a wine to match. That was so delicious, I signed up for the strolling-supper afternoon with jazz pianist Bob James, who paid tribute to Tap by naming a song after the restaurant on his *Dancing on the Water* CD, released in 2001. He played that and many other tunes on a baby grand as we strolled the grounds, dining on 80 different dishes, all amazing.

Peterson added al fresco dining on the patio a few years ago, with weather permitting, no reservations necessary, and an a la carte menu. It's leisurely and elegant, looking out at the manicured lawn and lovely St. Clair Lake.

As for libations, new cellar master Ron Edwards, formerly of Milford's Five Lakes Grill, stocks nearly 6,000 bottles and more than 500 selections from all over the world, including Chile, Australia and New Zealand, to match the eclectic menu, which changes daily.

Upcoming events in 2002 include the Garden Party with Bob James on Sunday, September 8, 2002 (tentative); and the American Chef's Dinner on Sunday, October 20 at 5 p.m.

# Taqueria Margarita

Opening a new restaurant can be a scary proposition the failure rate is as high as 85 percent, and most fail before one or two years are up.

That's why Miguel Osorio eased into the restaurant scene quietly, and on weekends only.

"I wanted to check the market to see what kind of food they like," says the 37-year-old owner of Osorio El Mexicano, a well-stocked Mexican specialty-foods store and unofficial gathering place for the Hispanic community.

Taqueria Margarita, just down from Osorio El Mexicano,
1319 W. South Airport Rd.,
Traverse City,
231-935-3712.
Open Wed.-Fri. 10:30-9, Sat.-Sun. 9-9.
Rating ✦✦

For the last year or so on Saturdays and Sundays, Osorio has rented out the restaurant space a few doors down from his store. The native Oaxacan serves a south Mexican-style menu, right down to the bottled-in-Mexico Coca-Cola, Sprite, 7-Up and Fanta.

Osorio says his Mexican customers like the 11.7-ounce bottles. "They taste a little different, too," he explains.

The restaurant has caught on in Traverse City, despite the tentative hours, and now is open Wednesdays through Sunday. From the moment you walk through the door, fresh cilantro and cumin fill the air, and despite the total absence of ambience, you know a good meal is coming by the aroma alone.

Chips arrive with two sauces, a mild green chile and a sensational hot red with chunks of avocado. The menu's heading reads "Taqueria Rinconcito Mexicano," a one-page offering of several types of soft-flour or corn-shell tacos, tamales, guacamole, teamed beef, eggs and chorizo, quesadillas, a trio of soups including beef, menudo and pozole, and for dessert, rice pudding and flan.

We tried the guacamole, which was creamy and spunky. Then a couple of tamales, one chicken and one pork, which were nice and toothy in texture, the mild yet fragrant flavor enhanced by the hot sauce with the avocado. Next, a couple of soft-flour sliced-steak tacos, which were punctuated with fresh cilantro and perfectly tender.

But the best dish of all—and all were excellent—was the barbacoa, or barbecue. It was beef steamed with mild peppers, bay leaves and cumin for four hours, shredded in a rich red sauce and served with rice and black beans. I'm still smacking my lips thinking about it.

We had no idea how much this would cost us—the menu neglected to list prices. But for all of that food, plus a couple of Cokes, the bill for two came to just $18.

Osorio's grocery store also has caught on—his clientele is about 40 percent non-Spanish-speaking, just folks coming in to find the great variety of chile peppers, spices, tortillas and other Mexican items that he carries.

# TC Hunan

This little strip-mall storefront restaurant off South Airport Road takes some effort to find (it's behind a Taco Bell) but is well worth the energy.

We passed a buffet as we entered the well-appointed restaurant, which was nearly empty on a Thursday night. Lovely Chinese flute music played in the background. The seating was comfortable. The table settings were elegant turquoise and red plates adorned with dragons. Our server was prompt and helpful. We salivated over the enormous menu, with six types of soup, 13 appetizers, and a vast list of entrees cooked Hunan style—hot and spicy—like I adore.

T.C. Hunan Chinese Restaurant, 1425 S. Airport Rd. in the 42nd St. Plaza, Traverse City; open daily 11:30 a.m.-2 p.m., lunch; 5 -8 p.m. Sun.-Thur.; 5:30 p.m.-8:30 p.m. Fri.-Sat.; Sunday 11:30 a.m.-3 p.m. Inexpensive. Rating ✦✦

We feasted on the best wonton soup I've eaten in ages—housemade broth that was redolent of chicken, fresh scallions and lemon grass over delicate little wrappers stuffed with seasoned pork. Then a light, crispy egg roll, and a great platter of orange-flavored chicken – tender and zesty, served over steamed rice. My husband ordered Hunan shrimp, medium hot, and it was steamed to perfection, surrounded by crisp pea pods and Chinese vegetables.

We ended up with a big doggy bag, enough food for a delicious dinner the next day. And it was divine.

# Terrace Room

Terrace Room,
McGuire's Resort, one
mile south of Cadillac
between M-115 and U.S.
131,
Cadillac,
231-775-9947
www.mcguiresresort.com.
Open 7 days a week for
breakfast, lunch and
dinner. Saturday buffet,
Sunday brunch.
Moderate to expensive.
Rating ✦✦✦

Surrounded by 6,000 acres of forest, the Terrace Room at McGuire's Resort offers fine dining and stellar hilltop views of the surrounding forest, Lake Cadillac and one of two golf courses at McGuire's. The menu features steaks, fresh fish and seafood, plus pastries and other confections from the on-site bakery.

The adjacent Curly's Bar and Grill, done up with knotty pine, lattice work and stained glass with shamrocks, brings lively evening and weekend entertainment and sandwiches, pizzas, fajitas, vegetarian entrees, salads and libations.

# Timmerin

Everything about this place whispers "class." From the brick patio to the inviting porch filled with white wicker furniture, the well-manicured landscaping to the stellar view of Crystal Lake, the white linen tablecloths to the attentive servers in black and white.

And most of all, the flawless cuisine.

Do I love Timmerin? Let me count the ways.

Open since the summer of 2001, the restaurant and bed and breakfast inn is a dream that was many years in the making. Mike and Donna Malecki bought the rambling 1907 cottage on Crystal Lake's east shore and moved their family of seven in Feb. 1990, starting in on renovations immediately.

Timmerin at The Inn at Beulah Beach, 173 Lake St., Beulah, 231-882-5523, Open May through October for dinner, 6-10 p.m., Mon.-Sat. (abbreviated hours off-season); Sun. brunch only, 11 a.m.-2 p.m. Full wine list. Expensive. Rating ✦✦✦✦

Now it's a cozy Victorian charmer, with an intimate main floor dining room, a small but efficient commercial kitchen, and two upper floors with beautifully appointed guests rooms, each with a sumptuous private bath and views of Crystal Lake. A new Garden Room, where a gazebo once stood, overlooks the creek that runs behind it and the lake in front.

Seven of us dined one fine evening at Timmerin, named for the executive chef, Tim White, and his wife, chef Erin Dankert, Donna Malecki's daughter. They met while at Vermont's New England Culinary Institute.

A soft summer breeze kept us cool at a big table on the wide, pillared porch as sunset approached. Other diners lingered inside the inviting Victorian dining room, which is painted a warm crimson and glows with golden wood floors and trim.

Chef White bills his all-made-from-scratch menu "new Michigan cuisine." His motto: "Simple's always better." It changes seasonally, but features starters such as jumbo lump crab salad with English cucumber, beets and fresh horseradish; creamy sweet corn soup with duck confit and chive oil; grilled shrimp salad with watermelon, prosciutto ham and watercress – which one of our table companions had as an entrée. If you want foie gras, it's here, seared and accompanying a Granny Smith waldorf salad with golden raisin puree.

White and Dankert have trained their service staff exceptionally well, right down to the fine art of napkin-folding. "That was a big thing," White says. "We brought people in and they hadn't had a lot of experience at this level, so we sat down with them for three days before we opened and went over every detail we could think of."

Indeed, our server waited on us hand and foot, returning again and again with fresh ciabatta bread, butter—Timmerin uses only the best-tasting Plugra—and refills for our drinks.

The tenderloin of beef is a dream—a thick medallion done to perfection, paired with a savory grilled mushroom ravioli, a sautee of spinach leaves and a port wine sauce that is pure poetry. The seared sea scallops are equally well prepared and beautifully presented, accompanied by a lovely purple potato, frisee and bacon salad with a luscious lemony caper-brown butter vinaigrette. Another entrée of note was the pan-seared salmon with new potatoes, baby French beans and a gorgeous pomegranate sauce. Other choices include grilled pork loin; sauteed duck breast; and artichokes, pasta and mushrooms with a truffled tomato broth.

If that weren't enough, the desserts are also stupendous. A baked and crisped Granny apple with caramel sauce and vanilla bean ice cream, a rich triangle of chocolate ganache with a milk-chocolate dipping sauce, and locally roasted Sundance coffee topped it all off. After a tour of the B&B upstairs, we walked along the shore, then behind the little cottages that make Beulah so appealing, happily full and not the least bit guilty for the calorie consumption.

And that, folks, is why they call it fine dining.

# Thunder Bay Resort

It is dusk, and the snow has taken on an icy shade of midnight blue. We have just come face to face with a wooly herd of Rocky Mountain bull elk, and now it is time for a five-course meal.

It is the ultimate winter indulgence—an elk-viewing sleigh ride and gourmet dinner at Thunder Bay Resort in Hillman, about 140 miles northeast of Traverse City.

After a chilly 45-minute deep-woods glide in a red 24-person sleigh pulled by two huge, handsome Belgian horses, we approach a cedar lodge in the middle of a forest whose windows glow with golden light. It is toasty inside, so we peel off our heavy coats, gloves and boots and drop our wool lap blankets by the massive floor-to-ceiling stone fireplace, which crackles with a roaring fire.

Thunder Bay Resort,
27800 M-32 E,
Hillman,
1-800-729-9375,
989-742-4956 or
www.thunderbaygolf.com.
Rates for the sleigh ride
and dinner start at $75
per person.
Rating ◆◆◆

The walls of the rustic, high-ceilinged log lodge are filled with moose, elk and deer heads, animal pelts, antiques and old handsaws. We head for our assigned tables, decked out in crisp linens and china, and begin the sumptuous feast, after wine or sparkling grape juice is poured. First course: shrimp cocktail and a rolled tartlet made with Macintosh apples and pears. Next: A cup of thick chicken noodle soup. Third course: a marvelously sweet sesame-flavored salad with Napa lettuce and crisp noodles. Fourth: A fork-tender roast crown of pork with roasted redskin potatoes. Last course: Michigan cherry coffee with hand-rolled Italian pizzelle waffle pastry stuffed with white chocolate mousse and drizzled with raspberry sauce.

What makes this event so spectacular is that our host, Jan Matthias, has prepared dinner for her 66 guests on two 100-year old gas/wood-burning stoves, a Detroit Jewel and a Garland. She's been making these meals for the last nine years, perfecting what is certainly a lost art and most definitely a trial-by-fire mission.

Nine years ago, in a previous cabin on the property, there was no electricity, so Matthias decided she'd go back to the old way of making a meal. Of course, no instructions came with the antique stoves she bought from a dealer. But Matthias, one of 13 siblings who grew up dirt poor on a farm between Hillman and Rust, recalled how her Polish mother, Anna Konwinski, prepared all of her family meals on a wood-burner.

"I saw her do it – it gave me a good idea of the firing-up process," says Matthias, who adds that her mom could cook anything and make it taste good.

"I probably ruined a good dozen meals before I perfected my method," she laughs. "You learn this was too hot or that was too long and that kind of thing. I mean, there are no dials to tell you what temperature that stove is—now I have it pretty much down to a science."

She single-handedly prepares two meals a day for between 88 and 132 people. Each crown roast, which she cooks for 3-1/2 hours, has about 25 ribs each—that's a whole lotta pork, and a ton of KP. Every plate is beautifully presented to boot.

But Matthias loves to put on a good show, and says that calling it a gourmet meal is actually a misnomer on the part of Thunder Bay, which she and husband Jack operate as a year-round ranch with lodging, cross-country skiing, sleigh rides, murder mystery weekends and golf.

"Truthfully, it is just good, wholesome, old-time cooking. Good ingredients, everything from scratch, old-style cooking."

Her recipes are available in a cookbook, *Flavor from the Village*, which Thunder Bay Resort sells in its gift shop.

# Trillium

I often brace myself when I go to a high-end restaurant. So many times, I have been utterly let down by poor service, overpriced food and underwhelming ambience.

Happily, that was not the case at Trillium in the Grand Traverse Resort. Given that it was my husband's birthday, even better.

Riding up the glass elevator to the 16th floor of the tallest building in the region felt like a great urban getaway. We easily could have been in Chicago or Toronto. As we entered the modern, glass-walled dining area and were seated by a window with a balcony and two-story ceiling above us, we looked out on a panorama of twinkling lights. Sunsets and day views are more spectacular, but the wide-open vista got us out of our cooped-up winter funk.

Our leather seats were comfortable, the small table was set with white linen and polished flatware, and a shiny silver lantern illuminated the space. At 7 p.m., we were among only two parties in the restaurant, and thus had blue-ribbon service. As the tables began to fill up, our server kept apace, prompt and professional as ever.

We started with a warm basket of moist white bread studded with dried cherries, then split a delicious Middle Eastern salad of roasted red and yellow beets with bulghur, tomato and parsley in a lemon vinaigrette. It was presented in a timbale shape, topped with a flower-shaped arrangement of red and green lettuce leaves and edged with smoky bacon bits.

Trillium in the Grand Traverse Resort and Spa, 100 Grand Traverse Village Blvd., Acme; 231-938-2100 or 800-748-0303. Dinner daily, 6-10 p.m. Sun.-Thurs. and until 1 a.m. Fri.-Sat. Reservations are recommended. Rating ✦✦✦

Our entrees were so outstanding, we were moaning with joy as we savored each bite. My husband's fork-tender Black Angus filet of beef was charbroiled and sat in a silky pool of veal demiglace with roasted garlic and shallots. It was accompanied by a salsa of sweet grilled corn, baby spinach, apple-smoked bacon and roasted red pepper and whipped potatoes with heavy cream, cheese and herbs, baked to a golden hue.

The birthday boy was in heaven.

Just as intricately flavored was my choice, a brine and fresh cranberry-cured pork tenderloin, marinated in fresh pineapple juice, honey and cranberry juice, pan-seared and crusted with toasted pecans and served with a veal demiglace and port-poached dried cherries. The melt-in-the-mouth medallions were arranged around tooth-crisp carrots, zucchini and creamy whipped potatoes.

"Nothing we do is that difficult," says 27-year-old chef de cuisine Christopher R. Mushall, a Traverse City native (T.C. High '93) who apprenticed at the five-star Princess in Scottsdale, Arizona, graduated from Johnson & Wales in Charleston, S.C. and studied at Schiller International in Engelburg, Switzerland. "It's back to simple – the kind of food that your mother or grandmother might have made."

Clearly, he is being humble—and he points out that his kitchen is staffed with foodies who love to turn out masterpieces. The Trillium's cooking style is classic French with Italian and Asian influences, although Mushall likes to say it is "fine Northern Michigan cuisine." He uses Maxbauer meats and applewood smoked bacon, and local produce and fish when available. It's a pricey place—our bill without alcohol came to $85 with tip—but worth it. This is not a stiff, formal restaurant by any means, despite the level of service. On the Tuesday night we visited, conventioneers were dressed in laid-back duds. After all, it's a resort.

"We want to keep it casual," says Mushall—we don't want to scare people away."

Trillium's wine list is extensive, with a few gaps that the restaurant is in the process of filling in.

# Villa il Ristorante Italiano

When I'm the mood for Italian food—something warm and wonderful, something soul-nourishing like a homey trattoria—I always think of my favorite restaurant in southwest Detroit, Giovanni's.

Why do I love that place? Because the minute I walk in, I am greeted with the pungent aroma of garlic. Because the food is authentic, well-priced and never disappointing. And because the owners, who are always on premises, make a point to walk around the room, greeting customers, finding out what they like and dislike, making a fuss over them, then doing the same at the next table. It's like one, big, happy family. Mangia!

> Villa il Ristorante
> Italiano, US 131 South,
> Petoskey,
> 231-347-1440;
> dinner only Mon.-Sat.
> 4:30-10:30 p.m.
> Rating ✦✦✦✦

That doesn't happen at too many restaurants. Maybe the owners are way too hurried and have too little help. Perhaps they perceive that customers might find that kind of attention obtrusive, and maybe they're right. But having experienced it in southwest Detroit and in Rome, Florence and Venice, I absolutely love such familiarity.

After a meal at Petoskey's Villa il Ristorante Italiano, and a later conversation with its owner, I think I may have found such a spot up north. It definitely has a Tuscan air to it, something owner Alex Czinki has been perfecting since 1976.

Czinki happens to be Hungarian, but don't let that throw you. He also happens to have grown up in Dearborn, not far from Giovanni's, in an area known for serving up the culinary wonders of Detroit's melting pot. Besides that, Czinki travels at least twice a year to Tuscany and has amassed such a collection of Italian wines—more than a thousand and ever-expanding—that his cellar has received the "Best of" Award of Excellence from *Wine Spectator* magazine many years in a row.

Villa il Ristorante Italiano is decorated with chianti bottles and baskets hanging from the rafters. The walls are rustic stucco, the tablecloths are red-checked and the exquisite two-story backlit stained-glass mosaic provides a brilliant focal point for the low-lit room. The noise level was good enough that all of us could hear each other, thanks to ample fabric in the seating and carpeting to dampen the sound.

For our first course, we chose a hearty Tuscan bean soup with pancetta and spinach, and a lovely couple of salads, one with prosciutto, walnuts, toasted onions and a crispy puck of baked Asiago cheese; the other, spinach salad with poppy seed dressing, bacon, pine nuts and Gorgonzola cheese.

The sea bass was firm and fresh, served with marinara atop lemon slices and garnished with Fontina cheese. The wild boar was tender — long-marinated in Chianti and rosemary, then simmered in bay leaves and juniper berries – and any gamey flavor was gone. That can be a plus for those who don't like wild stuff but somewhat disappointing for the hunter in our group who ordered it.

The gnocchi was rich, rich, rich—with handmade dumplings that are sautéed in vegetable oil and topped with a mushroom cream sauce – but what wasn't consumed at dinner was gleefully eaten the next day for lunch. I ordered the pasta sampler—lasagna, rigatoni and manicotti—all sensational, but I am still dreaming of the latter, rolled with a blend of four cheeses and baked with a creamy green onion sauce.

Even though we were stuffed, we ordered dessert, and we weren't sorry. A serving of chocolate-hazelnut gelato with a walnut-lace cup and a cannoli filled with ricotta and cream, topped with nuts and shaved chocolate sent us on our way, a couple of pounds heavier than we were going in.

We never saw Czinki that night, and that's a shame, because after a telephone conversation, he seems like a man who cares about his food and the vibes of his restaurant and thus would make the perfect host. He says some nights he's out, often acting as wine sommelier, but it's hard to run a business and greet guests at the same time.

I asked him about his pricing, which I found a couple dollars high on most dishes. His reply: "To get good people, you have to pay well." In turn, the customer pays a little extra, and that's fine with me. He says his turnover's low. And his Riedel Austrian crystal glassware is hand-washed. His bread is served with cannellini-bean pate, and what's more, his recipes include tons of garlic.

That's my kind of Italian restaurant.

# Walloon Lake Inn

Walloon Lake Inn,
on Winsor St., one
block west of M-75,
Walloon Lake Village,
231-535-2999
or 800-956-4665.
Open at 6 p.m. for
dinner, seven days a
week.
Expensive.
Rating ◆◆◆◆

This year-round restaurant and bed-and-breakfast inn looks like a big, knotty-pine-paneled Adirondack lodge, but the cuisine is anything but rustic. Chef David Beier's menu – classic French with Asian and Mediterranean touches—is as extraordinary as the view from this 110-year-old outpost, on the same lake where Hemingway spent his summers.

Fragrant cedars, pines and weeping willows frame the windows; outside, sunbathers lazily read books on the beach as boaters pull up at the dock for cocktails. Inside, the contrast of white linens, sparkling glassware and silver is soothing—and not the least bit stuffy—and the captain's chair seating is comfortable.

Appetizers such as bouchees au hommard—puff pastry with veal-tarragon-scented lobster—and entrees like fresh walleye, whitefish, filet with morels and other regional specialties are presented on pretty china, beautiful to the eye as well as the tongue.

Beier, who has worked in fine restaurants from the West Coast to Manhattan, says he doesn't miss the urban experience, which kept him cooped up without a home life for years. The outdoor life and personal bonds he's formed in northern Michigan "offer me the tranquility to face the kitchen, night after night." During fall, winter and spring, he offers an intimate, hands-on cooking school with lodging for foodies who aspire to his high level of cuisine and a taste of the rich yet simple life. It's $400 for four days.

# Whispers

I'd heard the menu at Shanty Creeks' Whispers restaurant was fabulous—but very expensive. I wanted to see if the long drive from Traverse City was worth it.

Located in the resort's $17-million Lodge at Cedar River, this 64-seat white-table-cloth restaurant has an intimate feel: softly lit, with soothing music and a cozy forest view. There are booths, a patio that overlooks the 18th hole of the Tom Weiskopf-designed Cedar River Golf Club, and a separate 24-seat dining room with a lake-blue wall.

Whispers
in the Lodge at Cedar River at Shanty Creek, Bellaire, 800-678-4111. Dinner only starting at 6 p.m. Closed during golf off-season in spring and autumn. Call for reservations. Expensive. Rating ✦✦✦✦

I love the paint job, in colors such as pumpkin, gold, gray-green and slate, with a design that flows like a river from the walls to the ceiling. Seats are comfortable and covered with art-nouveau prints. The light fixtures are subdued with whimsical fabric shades that look like golden lilies.

It's a casually elegant kind of place, perfect for resortwear, but worthy of better. Whispers' *raison d'être* is regional cuisine that takes advantage of local produce, organic when possible, with a seasonally changing menu executed by energetic executive chef Clifton Wilson. Guests can ogle its extensive wine collection in the glass-enclosed room off the dining area.

Wilson, 34 and a Charlevoix native, honed his culinary talents for several years as sous chef at the defunct Spencer Creek in Alden.

I was already psyched for a good meal, and was not disappointed. It was exquisite, from the attentive service to the quietude of the restaurant and its peaceful view. I started with a taste of smoked duck with fresh herbs, then a creamy layered strudel appetizer of smoked salmon with more herbs and greens. Next came a Pernod-imbued, light-cream soup—more like a bisque—of baby spinach and chicken broth and an orange and glazed-pecan salad with organic greens and orange-thyme vinaigrette. This was followed by an entree of char-grilled Black Angus tenderloin steak atop a chipotle polenta cake and black bean-corn salsa. I tasted my friend's plump, fresh seared sea scallops atop crisp pan-roasted potato medallions – delicious. My husband's peppered Alaskan halibut on coriander-scented jasmine rice was delicate and divine.

Each dish was beautifully plated, decorated with frilly, hand-cut garnishes of flowers, fruits and vegetables.

For dessert, try a bittersweet chocolate and black currant tart or any variation of crème brulee.

# Wildflower

I'm not much of a skier, but I was out on the trails for several hours one day at Crystal Mountain Resort in Thompsonville, falling and laughing more than I was gliding, and working up a powerful hunger.

So there I was, après ski, face to face with a massive buffet at Crystal's Wildflower Restaurant. To get to my table I had to pass a beautiful salad bar with great greens and crisp crudités, then a long stretch of covered chafing dishes filled with pasta, pork chops, whitefish Florentine, green beans in butter sauce with red peppers, spicy chicken nuggets with rice, and a carving station with fabulously scented prime rib. Not to mention an entire table heaped with pastries, cookies and cakes.

Wildflower Restaurant, Crystal Mountain Resort, 12500 Crystal Mountain Dr., Thompsonville, 231-378-2000 or 1-800-968-7686. Hours: Breakfast 6-11 a.m., lunch 11:30 a.m. - 2 p.m., dinner 5-9 p.m. Mon.-Thurs. 5-10- p.m. weekends. Buffets are served on weekends. Rating ✦✦✦

Who could resist?

The "on-a-diet" side of my brain was shouting that blood-curdling "Nooooo!" you hear in every cheesy movie. My dinner companions were already seduced by such an opulent, aromatic display.

Let's just suffice it to say I began rationalizing the ol' diet right out the window. After all, I worked off a ton of calories cross-country skiing, right? And having never been to this good-looking eatery, whose Arts and Crafts décor came right out of famed Scottish architect Charles Rennie Mackintosh's Willow Tea Room in Glasgow, I wanted to experience everything in the house.

I gave in to the spectacle of all that sauced-up splendor and needless to say, filled up several plates. One for salad, another for entrees, another for whatever didn't fit on the other two plates. I ate slowly, savoring each bite. The prime rib was first—very good, perfectly tender and juicy—accompanied by a zesty horseradish cream sauce. The beef tips and penne pasta were nicely seasoned. The fish was so-so. The chicken was spicy. The maple-glazed pork chop was the best of all.

Then I did a round at the dessert buffet: melt-in-the-mouth tea cakes, crisp peanut butter cookies, and a torte with raspberry filling and powdered sugar topping — moist, perfectly textured and not too sweet, just the way I like it.

Service was attentive and professional. Our plates were cleared and our drinks refilled just as we needed them, and the restaurant was quiet and casual.

But here's what I think: Off the menu is still the way to go. Well prepared as they were, most of the above-described dishes can be found most anywhere. And, as witnessed by my many platters, buffets and overeating go hand in hand.

What sets any restaurant apart from the pack are the extraordinary dishes, and the Wildflower has a wide-ranging and interesting menu of creative pastas, lots of fish and seafood and many other inventive-sounding entrees that have been orchestrated by executive chef Kristin Pyne. The Culinary Institute of America graduate is a Benzie County native who worked at Chicago's five-star/five diamond Four Seasons Restaurant and the Hyatt Grand Cypress in Orlando, Florida.

So next time I'm there, the first thing I'll do is look at the menu, and order straight.

# Windows

Its name suggests one reason to seek out this restaurant while up north—all of the windows offer a gorgeous view of the aqua-colored Grand Traverse Bay and the Old Mission Peninsula. And if you're lucky enough to catch the amber glow of a giant harvest moon in fall, be prepared for some serious moonlight.

The other reason, of course, is the first-class food chef-owner Phil Murray and his staff whip up year-round in the contemporary restaurant that is punctuated with soft lighting and a few well-placed antiques. The New Orleans-trained Murray, who worked at the Commander's Palace with famed chef Paul Prudhomme, imparts mouthwatering Cajun flare to his menu. For example, try the fork-tender filet of beef tenderloin blackened or chargrilled with spicy barbecued shrimp or, in season, the luscious, whisper-light blue lump crab puffs, dusted in French bread crumbs, then pan-sautéed in browned lemon butter.

Windows,
7677 SW Bayshore Dr.,
Traverse City;
231-941-0100.
Hours:
5-10 weekdays, 5-11 weekends. Early bird specials (before 5:30 p.m.) seven days a week.
Expensive.
Rating ✦✦✦

Dining room manager Mari Chamberlain thinks the secret to Murray's success is his commitment to quality: "Only the freshest and best ingredients," she says, such as one superb special, pan-sautéed walleye with a garlic cream sauce, sun-dried tomatoes and bay scallops. Top that off with the chocolate mousse Olivia, a marvel of dark chocolate, strawberries, raspberries, kiwi and whipped cream—and don't pass up the housemade truffles served with every check.

# Section Two

# Northern Michigan's Best Bets

# ARTISAN BREAD

Bay Bread Co.: Brenda Daray makes pricey but delicious baguettes, scones, cookies, cinnamon rolls and 35 varieties of specialty breads at this sparkling bakery near downtown. *601 Randolph St. at Maple, Traverse City; 231-922-8022. Hours: 7 a.m.-6 p.m. weekdays, 7-5 Sat. closed Sun.-Mon.*

Crooked Tree Breadworks: Greg Carpenter's ovens produce gorgeous rustic loaves and from-scratch pastries made with organic ingredients. *2264 M-119 Suite 5, Petoskey, 888-591-8688 or www.breadworks.com. Hours: 7 a.m. -6 p.m. Mon.-Sat. Breadmaking classes offered in winter.*

Pleasanton Brick Oven Bakery: Gerard Grabowski and Jan Shireman's sourdough loaves are moist and full of organic grains. *Manistee County, 231-864-2203. Available at L'Chayim in Beulah; Oryana Food Coop and the Saturday Farmer's Market in Traverse City; Bear Lake IGA; and Port City Organics on River St. in Manistee.*

Stone House Bread: Author and former TV newscaster Bob Pisor's sourdough delights are fabulously fresh—each loaf is dated so you can be sure. My favorites are the kalamata, the cherry-walnut, the North Country and the ciabatta. *407 South Main St., Leland, 231.256.2577, 800-252-3218 or www.stonehousebread.com. Also available throughout Northern Michigan.*

# BURGER BLITZ

Art's Tavern: For a juicy burger and a brewski with a big dollop of local color, this legendary watering hole is a Glen Arbor institution. *6487 W. Western Ave., Glen Arbor, 231-334-3754. 7 a.m.-2 a.m. No credit cards. Inexpensive.*

Boone's Long Lake Inn: This cavernous log lodge southwest of Traverse City features a cozy, rustic atmosphere, high-beamed ceilings, enormous slabs of steak, prime rib, and, of course, burgers. *7208 Secor Rd., Traverse City, 231-946-3991. Inexpensive.*

Boone's Primetime: Another rustic log cabin with a fireplace, small yet rambling, with juicy flame-broiled burgers and a hometown, everybody-knows-your-name ambience. *On St. Josephs in downtown Suttons Bay, 231-271-6688. Inexpensive.*

Brady's Bar: Another smoky place, this Olde Towne haunt was packed when I stopped by at lunchtime, but that didn't slow down the service, which was fast and fun. This classic paneled Irish pub features two pool tables, a hip jukebox and shamrock stained glass. And the bacon and cheddar burger is a melt-in-your-mouth masterpiece, served wrapped in a basket with chips and a pickle. *401 S. Union St., Traverse City; (231) 946-8153. Hours: 9-2 a.m. daily. Inexpensive.*

Dick's Pour House: This local bar was author Jim Harrison's hangout until he moved to Montana, but it still serves dandy homemade soups, great hamburgers — including the famous Plevalean cherry burgers — and pizza. *103 W. Phillips, Lake Leelanau, 231-256-9912. Inexpensive.*

Don's Drive-In: Sit in a booth, order a burger basket and milkshake and look out at East Bay while taking a romp back to the nifty-fifties, complete with nostalgic tunes on the jukebox. The circa-1958 classic diner serves up steaming ground-chuck burgers wrapped in paper with a huge order of fries and creamy coleslaw. *2030 U.S. 31 N., TC, 231-938-1860. Inexpensive.*

<u>Fischer's Happy Hour Tavern</u>: Local hangout in an old farmhouse with burgers, fish, homemade soups, pies and dressings. *M-22, between Northport and Leland, 231-386-9923. Inexpensive.*

<u>Joe's Friendly Tavern</u>: Big chuck-burgers, ground fresh daily in the rustic 50-year-old restaurant's butcher shop, $4 for the burger, $5.25 with fries, onion rings (my favorite) or cottage cheese. No credit cards. *11015 Front St., Empire, 231-326-5506. Inexpensive.*

<u>North Peak Brewing Co.</u>: The Black and Blue burger, charbroiled and topped with a nice pile of Gorgonzola cheese, is creamy and dreamy. Filling, too. I couldn't finish it. But I love the restaurant, with its brick walls, shiny wooden floors, towering ceilings and booths near the windows. It's fairly loud, even when the place is uncrowded. *400 W. Front St., Traverse City, 231- 941-7325. Inexpensive.*

<u>Rico's Café</u>: Decorated in deep greens with woodlands art, it's homey and comfy, the service is great, and there is enough privacy in the booths for meaningful conversation. The huge two-fisted 2/3-pound burger, chargrilled to perfection, is easily enough for two (but I ate most of it myself). *5790 US 31 South, Grawn, 2 miles west of Chum's Corner, 231-276-7070. Inexpensive.*

<u>The Suncatcher</u>: Truly a surprise to find such a grand burger-in-basket at the Cherryland Airport, but this is one to seek out, even if you aren't leaving on a plane anytime soon. The only hassle: Before you eat, you will have to go through the metal detector. No biggie unless you carry a lot of keys or other metal things on your person. Our friend was forced to go through the x-ray five times. As for the burger: Belissimo! Charbroiled, great bun, cheddar cheese...ahhhh. It's $4.95 for a 6-ouncer, add 60 cents for cheese. Watch the planes come and go. It's lovely. *1330 Airport Access Road., T.C. (upper floor), 231-941-0192. Inexpensive.*

<u>TC Traders</u>: A half-pound of choice ground sirloin for $4.95. It's seared, charbroiled and m-m-mouthwatering. Sit in the booth and pretend like you're in the galley of a tall ship. *1796 S. Garfield, TC, 231-929-9885. Inexpensive.*

# CHEESE

Inside the rough-hewn tasting room behind a wall of glass at Black Star Farms in Suttons Bay, John and Anne Hoyt make their award-winning Leelanau Cheese. Over a giant stainless-steel vat, they patiently stir the heated milk, cutting the curds with long strokes, turning them into a mellow, nutty artisan cheese called raclette. It's aged in a modern, temperature-controlled cave on the property and sells for $8-$10 a pound. They also make French-style fromage blanc (cheese spread) in plain, dill, garlic and peppercorn varieties at $3.50 per 8-ounce container.

The couple, who met during cheesemaking school in Switzerland, outgrew the converted gas station in Omena, where Leelanau Cheese Co. was born in '95. The gregarious Anne, who worked as a shepherd in her native France, says she doesn't mind people watching as they work — in fact, she rather enjoys it.

Leelanau Cheese Co., *10844 E. Revold Rd., Suttons Bay, 231-271-2600. Also available at Meijer's and Folgarelli's in Traverse City.*

# CHEESECAKE

It's called the home of the famous "Original Bite-size Cheesecake and Frozen Chocolate Dipped Cheesecake-On-A-Stick," but it's so much more. Lori Dawson and Mary Low whip up 47 tantalizing flavors of their delectable diet-busting cheesecakes in this Olde Towne eatery, and on a good day sell thousands of their bite-size babies. That's on top of 40 types of housemade soups (two versions daily) and fresh salads such as roasted chicken Caesar or spinach with apples and bacon. A 6-inch cheesecake is $15, a 9-inch is $25.

Underground Cheesecake Co., 406 S. Union St., Traverse City, 231-929-4418 www.undergroundcheesecake.com. 9 a.m.-5:30 p.m. Mon.-Fri., 9-3 Sat., closed Sun. Inexpensive to moderate.

# CHERRY FESTIVAL FOOD

With the ear-shattering backdrop of an F-16 doing power climbs and barrel rolls above the open space of the National Cherry Festival, French fry fiends were lined up 15 deep for Gibby's Fries, a concession that has been a fest favorite since 1946.

Bruce and Chris Hansen have operated the stand for 13 years. Their daughter Jennifer, niece Erica and other family members work inside the wagon, furiously filling orders. Bruce estimates they go through 1,000 pounds of potatoes on a good day.

The secret to their popularity? "We use only the best shortening— pure vegetable oil," explains Bruce, "we use only Idaho potatoes, and we never cook anything else in the same grease."

Gibby's spuds are about as thick as a baby finger. Bruce has an automatic cutter but he doesn't like the way they turn out, so every order is hand-cut, deep-fried to a golden brown and arrive in paper holders glistening in oil. They're good, greasy and cheap, considering the hard labor: $2 for a small – which is plenty for three people— and $3 for a large. Find them near the carny across from the Open Space. And don't forget to douse them in salt and malt vinegar for the full effect.

Then there's Mountain Spuds, one of a couple of concessions near the stained-glass store on the Parkway. Greg and Rebecca Abbott bought a machine made from a converted drill press from an inventor friend in West Virginia that turns an unpeeled russet or Burbank potato into a scalloped mass of thin slices in seconds. They're plunged into a 360-degree peanut-oil bath and emerge as a crisp, fun-to-eat pile of chips. Finish them with salt, malt vinegar, garlic and parsley salt or eat them plain. They're delicious.

"We're not trying to compete with Gibby's," Greg Abbott insists. It's a different product—much lighter." They're $2.50 for a giant portion. My favorite are the sweet potato chips – a bit pricey at $4 per portion, but a nice nod to health. Add a bit of salt and they're a sweet treat.

Next door, Tim Mikovitz is selling "fast and good" Moose Drool coffee from Missoula, MT. He's hoping to open his own place in Traverse City soon, so you can get a preview of his selection of premium espressos, cappuccinos, mochas, lattes and chai teas, which range from $1 to $3.50 a cup. He also carries Italian sodas for $3 – we liked the cherry and strawberry – and iced mochas.

Across the street in the Open Space, I loved the chicken quesadillas from Chianti's, nice and cheesy-spicy with bits of chicken, jalapenos and red peppers. My husband got Chianti's Philly Cheese Steak. He grew up in the Philadelphia area and says that on a scale of 1 to 10, it ranked right up there with an 8 or 9. National Cherry Festival is held the first or second week in July in Traverse City.

# CHERRY AND OTHER FRUIT PRODUCTS

American Spoon Foods, 411 East Lake St., Petoskey, 231-347-1739; 315 Bridge St., Charlevoix, 231-547-5222; 230 East Front St., Traverse City, 231-935-4480; Grand Traverse Resort, Traverse City, 231-938-5358; 245 East Main St., Harbor Springs, 231-526-8628. General info: 800-222-5886; www.spoon.com.

Amon Orchards, 8066 US 31 N, PO Box 27, Acme, 800-937-1644 or 231-938-9160, www.amonorchards.com.

Benjamin Twiggs, 1215 E. Front St., Traverse City, 877-236-8944, www.benjamintwiggs.com.

Brownwood Acres, at the north end of Torch Lake on US-31, Eastport, 877-591-3101 or 231-599-3101, www.brownwoodacres.com.

Cherry Hut, 246 US 31, Beulah, 231-882-4431, Home of the original smiley face and fabulous pies. www.cherryproducts.com.

Cherry Republic, a virtual nation of products, at 6026 S. Lake St., Glen Arbor, 800-206-6949, www.cherryrepublic.com.

Cherry Stop, which recently quadrupled its space in this new location, at 211 E. Front St., Traverse City, 800-286-7209, 231-929-3990 or www.cherrystop.com.

Engle Ridge Farm, featuring Michigan Balaton cherry products, at 6754 Yuba Rd., Williamsburg, 888-448-5817. www.engleridgefarm.com.

Kilcherman's Christmas Cove Farm, with more than 50 different antique and historic apples, gift baskets, cider; open mid-September through first weekend in November, 11573 N. Kilcherman Rd., Northport, 231-386-5637.

Leland Cherry Co., 106 Lake St., Suite 2, Leland, 800-939-3199, 231-256-2033, www.lelandcherry.com.

Rocky Top Farms, featuring blueberry and cherry butters and strawberry preserves; on Essex Rd. near Ellsworth, 800-862-9303 or 231-599-2251.

# CHOCOLATE TOUR

Chocoholics looking for a rainy-day activity up north will have a swell time at the Kilwin's Chocolate factory, where large and small groups are led through tours, presumably salivating all the way. Visitors are escorted through a surprisingly small kitchen, considering its daily output of up to 700 pounds of sweets. It's where they make all the centers, such as cremes and caramels. Once the caramels are hardened, they're cut up into squares and put on a big motorized, refrigerated belt called an enrober, which also coats the bottoms of the candies. Then it passes under what Kilwin's calls a chocolate waterfall. Mmmm. The whole tour takes about 15 minutes. Luckily, there's a small retail shop at the end, where the exquisite chocolates go for $16-$22 a pound. Hey, who needs the beach?

The Kilwin's tour is free. It's at 355 N. Division Rd. (go east through town up the E. Mitchell hill). Tours are Mon.-Thurs. at 10:30 and 11 a.m. and 2 and 2:30 p.m. Call 231-347-3800 for more information or visit www.kilwins.com. Other locations all over the north.

# COFFEEHOUSES/DELIS/CAFES

American Spoon Gelato Café opened July 2001 in Petoskey. In 2002, the company's 20th anniversary, full table service was added to this gleaming black-and-white café, whose famed New York chef, Larry Forgione, has developed a divine menu. Breakfast, soups, salads, sandwiches (the grilled Angus beef panini with smoked mozzarella, red onions, arugula, red spoon peppers and barbecue mustard is fab), bruschetta, pasta — and of course, gelato, the thick, yummy Italian ice cream, as well as fruit-flavored sorbetto. Try the chocolate toasted almond gelato with a cup of cappuccino. That's amore. *413 East Lake St., Petoskey, 231-347-7004. Find gelato and sorbetto in the Traverse City location at 230 East Front St., Traverse City, 231-935-4480.*

L'Chayim Deli: This Big Apple-style deli serves up enormous sandwiches on great bread and all kinds of specialty foods, salads, bagels, desserts and cappuccino. *274 S. Benzie Blvd., Beulah, 231-882-5221.*

Cherry Hut: Jerry, the Cherry-Faced Pie Boy, whose smiling red countenance rises above this roadside restaurant as a kitschy summer beacon, just might be the world's first smiley face — it has marked this roadside fruit stand since 1922. Leonard and Brenda Case bought it in 1959 and have served its famous cherry pies to generations of hungry vacationers ever since. It also features a full, all-American lunch and dinner menu. "We have traditional food," says Leonard. "We haven't gone to the trendy or anything French." There's no bar, just coffee, tea, soft drinks and frosted cherry-ade. And of course, cherry ice cream. *246 US 31, Beulah, 231-882-4431, www.cherryproducts.com.*

Fieldstone Deli: I lust for their pepperoni bread, made fresh daily and filled with basil pesto and ample pepperoni. Their chicken-mushroom and roast beef-horseradish wraps are good, too, among the many deli sandwiches they offer, and their pizza is to die for. *7270 N. Long Lake Rd., Traverse City, 231-922-7712. Open 8 a.m.-10 p.m. daily.*

Horizon Books Shine Café: In the lower level of this beloved, people-friendly bookstore, find a coffee bar (there's one upstairs, too), salads and sandwiches, desserts, many tables, a fireplace and eclectic groups that meet for conversation, live music and just plain mingling. *245 E. Front St., Traverse City, 231-946-7290. Hours 7 a.m.-11 p.m. daily.*

Leelanau Coffee Roasting Co.: Steve and Jon Arens roast more than 90 international beans at this Glen Arbor java emporium and offer other coffee-related food items. *6443 Western Ave. (M22), Glen Arbor, 800-424-JAVA. www.coffeeguys.com or www.leelanaucoffee.com.*

Mustard's: The menu is spicy and innovative – deli-style sandwiches and wraps, salads and soups – and the ingredients are fresh and delicious. Its fine-dining parent, Amical on Front Street, has never disappointed me, and Mustard's, whose menu boasts "fine sandwiches," delivers on its promise. Belly up to the counter and order a Jamaica Joe wrap with jerk chicken breast, tomatoes, onion and ranch dressing or a big third-pound Angus burger with mozzarella and pesto. Any number of vegetarian selections — yummy and large, enough to share. *202 E. State St., Traverse City, 231-929-0700. Lunch Mon.-Fri. 11 a.m.-5 p.m., Sat. noon-5 p.m. Full-service breakfast is Mon.-Fri. 7-11 a.m., Sat. 7-noon. Closed Sun. Inexpensive.*

Ray's Coffeehouse: The place to hang, sip coffee or latte, read a magazine and hear what's happening around town. It's where the kool kats congregate in T.C. *129 E. Front St., 231-929-1006. Inexpensive.*

Roast & Toast, Petoskey: Good java and decent soups, salads and desserts. Entertainment also featured in this cheery coffeehouse. *309 E. Lake St. (231) 347-7767.*

Salt City Café: Friendly proprietor Shawn Barch serves cappuccino, mochas, lattes and fresh baked goods such as his sinful cinnamon rolls in the exposed-brick, high-ceilinged Briny Building, a restored gem a block off River Street in the historic downtown area. *50 Filer Street, Suite D, Manistee, 231-398-9343. Inexpensive.*

Silver Swan: The falafel plate with hummous, baba ghanoush and tabbouleh salad for $7.95 is simply mah-velous. Chef Yola Pepellashi, a Grosse Pointe native of Albanian-German heritage, sisters Erika and Petra and cousin Elton all work here, making other entrees and killer desserts such as cream puffs, strawberry shortcakes, triple chocolate walnut brownies and Napoleons as well as gift baskets. Silver Swan also features imported eclectic gifts such as hand-carved wooden spoons from Kenya, jewelry from Nepal, beaded bags from Tibet, Polish crystal and hand-made paper journals. This eatery seats 20 people, or get a carryout. Call ahead for the felafel; it's a special. *13692 SW Bay Shore Dr., 231-932-0203; open 11 a.m.-8 p.m. Mon.-Fri., closed weekends. Inexpensive.*

Silvertree: Vicki and Matthew Walheim's chicken salad on croissant or baguette is as fresh and savory as any I've eaten in Paris – and I've wolfed down a few. The housemade soups, interesting salads and the inspirational Geneva Mae gourmet cheesecakes, whichthey produce on-site, are fabulous, too. The owners hail from the Excalibur restaurant in Southfield, MI. *305 N. St. Josephs in Suttons Bay, 231-271-2271; hours: 11-7 p.m. Mon.-Fri., 11 a.m.-4 p.m. Sat.; hours vary in winter. Inexpensive.*

Trick Dog Gallery/Café: Elberta artist Greg Jaris and wife Linda named their eclectic work-in-progress café after their Pointer-mix Sadie and adopted dog, Trick. They serve up art with espresso, coffee, smoothies, Italian sodas, Chai tea, French toast, iced babka toast or brown bread with Mascarpone cheese, Cuban sandwiches and fresh baked goods. Find works by Jaris, Woody Jones, Jerry Berta and Brian Confer, along with gifts, toys, dog products and clothing. In Elberta, overlooking Betsie Bay. *Take M-22 into Elberta Village and turn right at the curve. Follow Furnace Rd. along the bay. The gallery is on the left about a mile down. 231-352-TDOG. Memorial Day-Labor Day open 9-5 daily; abbreviated hours off-season.*

# DESIGNER MILK

At Shetler's Amazing Graze Farm, Sally and George Shetler's 40 cows feed on organic pastures and produce milk the old way — "pasteurized, not homogenized, so it separates like old-fashioned milk," says Sally.

Shetler's milk products — in whole (4%), skim and fat-free — also come in old-fashioned glass bottles. There's also a rich 4% version of chocolate milk that is comparable to a creamy shake, and for those who want to whip up a fabulous old-fashioned dessert, try Shetler's heavy cream.

Shetler's Family Dairy, *5436 Tyler Rd., 6 miles east of Kalkaska off M-72. Hours: Mon.-Sat. 10-2;* also at Burritt's, Edson Farms, Folgarelli's, Maxbauer's Meats and Oryana in Traverse City; Hanson's in Suttons Bay; Cindy's Farm, Galley Gourmet, the Grain Train and Pond Hill Farm in Petoskey; at Tapawingo restaurant in Ellsworth and Rocco's restaurant in Kalkaska.

# FARM MARKETS

Amon Orchards: This family-friendly spot offers summer trolley rides, a petting farm and a bakery. July: Cherries, peaches, blueberries, raspberries. August: Cherries, apples, blueberries, raspberries. September and October: pumpkins, squash, gourds. Family Fall Festival October weekends. *8066 US 31 North, Williamsburg, 231-938-1644.*

Bibb's Manitou Market: On-site bakery; coffee, beer and wine; outdoor seating. Open May - October. *3 miles south of Leland on M 22, next to Good Harbor Vineyards, 231-256-7550.*

Buchan's Blueberry Hill: Blueberries August to October; peaches in August; apples in mid-September. Open July-October. Closed Sunday. *1472 Nelson Road Traverse City, 231-223-4846.*

Busha's Brae Herb Farm: Fresh herbs, seasonings and herbal products. *Suttons Bay; by appointment only, 231-271-6284.*

Chrissy's Farm Market: Fruits, vegetables, homemade pies and bread, local crafts, flowers. Open daily April-November. *7846 US 31 South, Interlochen, 231-276-9030.*

Covered Wagon Farm Market: Pies, baked goods, jams and jellies all seasons. Asparagus in mid-May, strawberries in mid-June, cherries in mid-July, apples and cider the end of August and in September, pumpkins in October. Christmas trees, handmade wreaths and garlands in December. Open May - December (closed part of November). *8996 M-204 (also known as E. Duck Lake Rd.) Suttons Bay, 231-271-6658.*

Dan's Market and Garden Center: Fruit, vegetables, plants, flowers, baked goods. Open all year. *2415 N. Garfield Ave. Traverse City, 231-946-8685.*

DeKorne Apiary: The DeKorne beekeeping and honey-processing farm has been in operation for four generations. Visitors can watch as honey is extracted at their farm from August-October. The 5 - pound honey in a jar sells for $8. Call ahead. *On 10758 Essex Rd. near Ellsworth; 231-588-6062.*

**Elzer Farm:** Cherry pies and jam, greenhouse, U-pick asparagus in May, strawberries in mid-June, cherries in mid-July, raspberries in July and August, apples from end of August through September, pumpkins in October. Open daily, May - Sept. *12654 Center Rd., Traverse City, 231-223-9292.*

**Friske Orchard:** Apples, cherries, peaches, apricots, nectarines and strawberries. Fruit stand, bakery, market with crafts. *10743 N. US 31 in Atwood, 231-599-2604.*

**Flying Scotts' Farm:** Cherries in July and August. *M 204 Suttons Bay, 231-271-3871.*

**Gallagher's Farm Market:** Sweet cherries, fresh fruits and vegetables, baked goods, jam and jellies. U-pick cherries in July and August. Open June-October. *7237 M 72 West Traverse City, 231-947-1689.*

**Glen Brown's Fruit Stand:** Sweet cherries, July and August. Apples, peaches, pumpkins, cider and caramel apples. Open June-October. *5300 N West Bayshore Dr., Omena, 231-386-5855.*

**Harbor Hill Fruit Farm:** Cherries, apples, apricots, peaches, plums. *1742 Schomberg Rd. 3 miles south of Leland, Lake Leelanau 231-256-7666.*

**King's Orchards:** U-pick sweet and sour cherries in July, apricots in August, peaches in mid-August, apples in September. Strawberries, vegetables and sweet corn from stand. *4620 N. M 88 Hwy., Central Lake, 231-544-6479.*

**Leelanau Farmers' Markets:** Fresh produce, food items, crafts and more, summer-fall. *At the Ice Skating Park in Suttons Bay and next to the Empire Post Office from 8 a.m.-noon Sat., and at the Bluebird Parking Lot in Leland 8-11:30 a.m. Tues.*

**Lighthouse Market:** Peaches and blackberries, picked and U-pick. Call ahead, *17083 Center Rd., Old Mission, 231-223-9212.*

**Omena U-Pick Cut Flowers:** More than 50 varieties of perennials and annuals. *M-22, 1 mile south of Omena, 231-271-6432.*

<u>Traverse City Farmer's Market</u>: Fruits, vegetables, plants, flowers and baked goods offered every Saturday mid-May through October. Wednesdays starting the 3rd Wednesday of July through September. *North of downtown parking lot off Grandview Parkway, 231-922-2090.*

# ICE CREAM

Next time you sidle up to a sliding window on a hot day with a craving that can only be quelled with an ice cream cone, consider the life of the person on the other side of the glass. During high season here in resortland, an ice cream vendor works an average 12-hour day, seven days a week, serving customers nonstop when the temperatures soar, and none if the weather's chilly.

<u>Moomer's</u>: My favorite. Nancy and Bob Plummer scoop about 700 cones of their luscious handmade, hard-packed Moomer's ice cream a day, and another 300 specialty items such as banana splits, turtle sundaes, Cowpies and Udder Delights. Top-selling flavors are vanilla, butter pecan, chocolate peanut butter, turtle cheesecake, and coconut-almond delight. Come before 7 p.m. if you don't want to stand in line, advises Bob, who also offers $3-per-person hayrides and tours of their farm just west of Twin Lakes Park; they've booked more than 1,300 day trips this year. Moomers products also are available at Grand Traverse Pie Co., Cuppa Joe, Bowers Harbor Inn, North Peak Brewing Co. and Suncatchers at the Cherry Capital Airport in Traverse City; Chateau de Leelanau Vineyard & Winery, the Covered Wagon Market and the Ice Cream Factory in Suttons Bay; Leelanau Country Inn in Maple City and Art's Tavern in Glen Arbor. *Moomers Homemade Ice Cream, 7263 N. Long Lake Rd., 231-941-4122, noon-10 p.m. daily in season.*

<u>Dairy Bar:</u> The little window opened last year and gets traffic from people taking the zoo tunnel. I like the chocolate-dipped soft-cone, which is also offered as a cherry dip. On a busy day, sundaes, slushes and 400-plus cones fly out the window. *Behind the Mackinaw Brewing Co. at Front and Cass. hours are 11 a.m.-10 p.m. daily; 231-933-1100 for the brewery.*

<u>Bardon's:</u> Lines form in front of Bardon's before it even opens for the day, which delights owners Pete and Sharon Bentley. They've been operating the 50-year-old Wonder Freeze at Front and Garfield for 16 years, and they use a premium brand of chocolate for their soft-cone dips that is positively dreamy. Pete says they sell a steady stream of about 300 cones a day, 160 hotdogs, 130 shakes and many hard-packed cones to the sports teams and other regulars who scream

ice cream all summer long. *Bardon's, 1100 E. Front, 231-941-4326, 11-10 daily.*

<u>Dairy Lodge:</u> I love the nifty-fifties logo of the Dairy Lodge on Division between Front and the Parkway, where Carol Popp and her husband Raymond do a brisk 300-cone day and have a huge following for their creamy chocolate malts, Flurries, splits and Hot Fudge Brownie Royales. Their nondairy Dole Whips are catching on with a growing number of lactose-intolerant customers. The Popps have owned the 50-something Lodge for 17 years, and thanks to what Carol calls "prompt, conscientious, happy employees who have returned year after year," they don't mind the time commitment.

"It's a wonderful retirement project for us," she says. But for those dreaming that an ice cream stand could be their ticket to summers off — don't bank on it, she says. *Dairy Lodge, 405 N. Division, 941-4374; 11-11 until Labor Day, shorter hours after that.*

Other great T.C. ice cream spots: <u>Kilwin's</u>, *129 E. Front, 946-2403,* and the <u>Dairy Queen</u>, *3200 S. Airport, 935-4333; and at 1660 U.S. 31 N., 938-0441.*

# FOODIE HEAVEN

Any time I'm looking for an unusual ingredient for a recipe, I know exactly who to call. Folgarelli's on Front St.

The long, narrow, old-fashioned wood-floored store is housed in a 125-plus-year-old former train station in Traverse City. I've never seen it when it wasn't packed with people. If there's a wait, it's often because customers are chatting with each other, swapping food information, or finding out about one of the zillions of items the store stocks from a well-informed staffer.

"I've worked here 10 years and I'm still finding new things in this store," says store manager Judy Bialy.

It's foodie heaven, a hangout for cooks and eaters, chefs and feeders.

A case in point: I was making a recipe that called for salt-cured capers. I'd never seen or heard of them, but I wanted to see what the buzz was all about. I called Folgarelli's, and they carried them at the deli counter. They also sell loose pine nuts, not the premeasured, high-priced packages I usually find in supermarkets. I can buy a couple of tablespoons if I want.

The store also carries some other amazing things for a small town like T.C.: Pureed mango, pickled ginger, salted cod, pasta sauce with sardines, and Rao's and Patsy's pasta sauces from New York. There are Asian delectables like miso, fish sauces, coconut milk and cellophane noodles, beans from all over the world and fresh pasta noodles made on premises. Plus a huge selection of olive oils and balsamic vinegars, and several types of butters such as ultra-rich Plugra, President's, and one from France, Isigny Ste. Mere.

I got to talking to Terri Collins behind the cash register, and two men who were standing in line, and we all got into a rousing discussion of the great crusty loaves of bread in the window – the dough is from Nancy Silverton's LaBrea Bakery in L.A., and Folgarelli's bakes it fresh daily. We all started talking about food and recipes. The men were father and son, Vince and Mike DePaulis. Vince, the

father, lives on the east side of the state in Millersburg. His son
Mike had moved here from downstate recently to start Northville
Catering Co. They were at Folgarelli's to stock up on goodies and
have a father-son reunion. Mike said he'd send me some recipes. I
can't wait to see them.

See? Folgarelli's is like that. You never know whom you'll meet,
but you know you have a big thing in common. Food is the univer-
sal language.

And those salt-cured capers? The recipe said they would impart
scents of exotic flowers and herbs to my pork dish, nuances never
hinted at by vinegar-packed capers. The recipe was right on. Soak
them in water for 10 minutes and drain, and they are heavenly.

Folgarelli's, which also offers gift baskets, party catering and divine
carryout deli salads and sandwiches, is at 424 W. Front St.; 231-941-
7651. Hours: 9:30 a.m.-6:30 p.m. Mon.-Fri., 9:30 a.m.-5:30 p.m. Sat., 10
a.m.-4 p.m. Sun.

Other foodie hangouts:

Burritt's Market: Wonderful butcher shop, fine wines, gourmet
goodies. 509 W. Front St., Traverse City, 231-946-3300. Hours: 9 a.m.-7
p.m. Mon.-Sat.; closed Sun.

Carlson's Fish Market: Next door to Burritt's is this sparkling seafood emporium, with smoked and fresh local catches from the family business that put Leland's Fishtown on the map. 511 W. Front St.,
Traverse City; 231- 941-9392

Hansen Foods: This grocer caters to appreciative customers with
more than 500 wine selections, fresh produce, an amazing bakery
and hot deli, Black Angus Beef and even homemade hot dogs. 91 4th
Street, Suttons Bay, 231-271-4280. 231-271-4280

<u>Mary's Kitchen Port:</u> This jam-packed kitchen and specialty-foods store carries everything from designer sea salt to Silpat baking sheets. The carryout salads and sandwiches are fabulous. *539 W. Front St., 231-941-0525.*

<u>Maxbauer's Meats:</u> An old-fashioned market with divine meats and seafood. Try the hunter's sausage — it's yummy. *407 S. Union St. in Olde Towne, 231-947-7698.*

<u>Pleva's Meats:</u> Ray Pleva's been on *Oprah* and *Home Improvement*, tirelessly promoting all things cherry. That's why he's known around these parts as Mr. Cherry, for his cherry sausages and low-fat Plevalean burgers. Buy it and other innovative cherry things at this Leelanau County market at *8974 S. Kasson St., Cedar, 231-228-5000 or www.plevas.com.*

<u>The Blue Goat:</u> Formerly The Village Wine Shoppe, find a great selection of wines, champagne and gourmet items. *875 E. Front St., Traverse City. 231-941-9463.*

<u>Wine Country Market:</u> Interesting wines and edibles. *541 W. Front Street, Traverse City. 231-935-17768. Hours: Mon.-Sat. 10-7.*

# PIES

Shortly after our move to Traverse City in 1999, we found a huge boxed pie at our front door with a note from our neighbor, welcoming us to paradise, as he so eloquently put it. It was our first taste of the amazing treats that are baked at Grand Traverse Pie Company—a big, crusty, cinnamon-scented apple pie. And it was the first time in our married life that anyone ever acknowledged our move to any neighborhood.

Mike and Denise Busley made the pie at their Front Street shop. It's the Busleys sixth year in Traverse City, a place they moved to from San Diego after researching their options. They wanted to get out of the big city and all the congestion that goes with it, find a good place where they could raise their kids – Kelly and Bobby – and they have no regrets.

Mike, a Lansing native and former engineer, and Denise, who worked in medical sales, borrowed their recipes and learned the business from owners of a successful San Diego pie company. They bake a long and luscious list of fresh-fruit and cream pies every day, using local ingredients sweetened with sugar and thickened with flour (never canned gels or mixes), and made-from-scratch-daily dough.

"It's a lot more manual labor than I'm used to," says Mike, "but it's good work, very satisfying, and I bring the kids in to help."

Grand Traverse Pie Company, 525 W. Front St., 231-922-7437. Hours: Mon.-Fri. 9 a.m.-5:30 p.m., Sat. 9-5, closed Sun. Pies are around $10 each.

Another good pie:

The Cherry Hut: A kitschy vintage roadside restaurant with delicious cherry pies, preserves, ice cream, juice and other cherry treats. 246 US 31, Beulah, 231-882-4431, www.cherryproducts.com. Pies are $5.95 or three for $15.

# PIZZA

Like everywhere in America, this food dominates Northen Michigan menus. Here are a few spots that stand out.

Mr. Mike's Detroit Pizza: Owner Mike Malinowski offers two types of Detroit pizza – the downriver Detroit style of my youth and the Buddy's-style version of my coming-of-age. It's a small place with a maize-and-blue theme (a tribute to the Wolverines), Red Wings memorabilia on the walls, and enough room for 16 diners. We jammed in with nine people the other night, and they had run out of dough for the round version, so we tried the Buddy's style and it was superb.

Malinowski formerly owned Mr. Mike's Deli & Pizzeria in Warren. He and brothers John and Todd and their parents Marion and Shirley are partners in the Traverse City restaurant as well as another outside the Las Vegas strip in Nevada. For nearly 20 years, from 1970-89, the family owned Fiore's Lounge in Sterling Heights, which is where Mr. Mike says he learned how to cook. He also did quite a bit of sleuthing around the original Buddy's to find out just what it is that makes those crusts so delicious. "The trick is what you oil your pans with," he says, "but that's a secret."

The Shirley Special Supreme with "the works" is a good bet, as is the Bay View with sausage, tomatoes and garlic. Prices are $15-$20 for a large deep-dish (16 pieces) and $11 for an eight-slice round-crust pie with one topping. There's no bar, and soft drinks are $1.50 from the fountain and include one refill.

Mr. Mike's is at 920 N. U.S. 31; 231-922-7141. Carryout and delivery available. Hours: 11 a.m.-10 p.m. Mon.-Sat., closed Sun.

Other good bets: Fieldstone Deli, (see page 145), Paesano's Pizza, 447 E. Front St., Traverse City, 231-941-5740; and Rico's Café in Grawn (see page 138).

I'll have an expanded pizza section in next year's edition.

# THE WINERIES

## Leelanau County

Bel Lago Vineyards and Winery: These picturesque vineyards over-look Lake Leelanau and Lake Michigan and produce Pinot Grigio, Chardonnay, Pinot Noir, Riesling, Gewürtztraminer, Leelanau Primavera and a variety of other still and sparkling wines. *Tasting Room. Open May - October. 6530 S. Lake Shore Dr., 7 miles south of Lake Leelanau, Cedar, 231-228-4800.*

Black Star Farms: At this agritourism spot, find white, red and fruit and sparkling fruit juices. European vinifera grape varieties are fea-tured along with the award-winning "Arcturos" line. There's a bed and breakfast inn and a cheesemaking facility in the tasting room. *10844 E. Revold Rd., Suttons Bay, 231-271-4884.*

Boskydel Vineyards: Overlooking Lake Leelanau, it specializes in dry to semi-dry table wines made from hybrid varieties, including Soleil Blanc, Vignoles, and other dry and semi-sweet whites. Its reds include De Chaunac, Roi Des Rouges, Rose Du Cru, Rose De Chaunac and De Chaunac Rose, all estate-bottled. No credit cards. *7501 E. Otto Rd. Lake Leelanau, 231-256-7272.*

Chateau de Leelanau: The only all-female owned and managed win-ery this side of the Mississippi. Cardiologist Roberta Kurtz and Joanne M. Smart are the owners, Karen Piaskowski handles sales and marketing and Bonnie Supina runs the tasting room. Winemaker Chris Guest is the solo fellow. *5048 S. West Bay Shore Dr., M-22 and Hilltop Road just south of Suttons Bay, 231-271-8888.*

Chateau Fontaine: Try wine from Chardonnay, Riesling and Pi-not Gris grapes as well as cherry wine. Tasting room is open May-October. *2290 S. French Road on the west side of Lake Leelanau, 231-256-0000.*

Ciccone Vineyard & Winery: Singer Madonna's dad Tony owns this winery. Tasting and tours are by appointment Thursday-Sun-day. Take in a picturesque panorama of the west arm of Grand

Traverse Bay and Leelanau Peninsula while sipping Gewürztraminer, Cabernet Franc, Pinot Noir, Chardonnay or Rose d' Cabernet wine. *10343 E. Hilltop Rd., Suttons Bay, 231-271-5551.*

Good Harbor Vineyards: Wines include Trillium, Fishtown White, Chardonnay, Riesling, Pinot Gris, Pinot Noir, Moonstruck Brut (champagne), Northern Lights, Manitou and Cherry. All have won medals at the Michigan State Fair and Tasters Guild International wine judgings. Take a self-guided tour or a free tasting. Open May-November. *34 S. Manitou Trail off M-22, three miles south of Leland, Lake Leelanau, 231-256-7165.*

L. Mawby Vineyards: Larry Mawby makes *Methode champenoise* sparkling wines and white table wine, including Vignoles and Sandpiper. His Cremant Brut and Talisman Brut won silver medals in world competition. Open May-October. Also hosts seasonal catered picnics and events. *4519 S. Elm Valley Rd., Suttons Bay, 231-271-3522.*

Leelanau Wine Cellars: Drop by for a full line of vinifera, hybrid and fruit wines, tours and tastings with a tasting room that overlooks West Grand Traverse Bay. The vineyard won three bronzes, a silver and a gold medal (for 1996 Chardonnay Grand Reserve) at the Michigan State Fair. Open June-October. *12683 E. Tatch Rd., left off M 22, Omena, 231-386-5201.*

Raftshol Vineyards Inc.: This new-in-1999 winery and tasting room features Bordeaux varietal red wines including Merlot, Cabernet Sauvignon and Cabernet Franc as well as Chardonnay, Riesling and Gewürztraminer white wines. *1865 N. West Bay Shore Dr., 2.5 miles north of Suttons Bay and 1 mile south of the Leelanau Sands Casino on M-22, Suttons Bay, 231-271-5650.*

Shady Lane Cellars: Set in a historic, restored fieldstone building, it produces *methode champenoise* sparkling wines. Its 1994 Brut won a gold medal at the 1998 Michigan State Fair. Also features Rieslings, Pinot Noirs and Chardonnays. Open May-October. *9580 Shady Lane, 8 miles north of Traverse City in Suttons Bay, 231-947-8865.*

Willow Vineyards: Spectacular views of West Grand Traverse Bay can be had from its tasting room. It produces Chardonnay, Pinot

Noir and Pinot Gris. *10702 East Hilltop Rd., 9 miles north of Traverse City in Suttons Bay, 231-271-4810.*

# Old Mission Wineries

Bowers Harbor Vineyards: Otis and Oakley, the family dogs, greet visitors to this tasting room with Michigan-made gifts and crisp, dry "unwooded" Chardonnays, Pinot Gris, sparkling Riesling and spiced cherry wine. Open year-round; January 1-April 1, weekends only. *2896 Bowers Harbor Rd. between Center Rd. and Peninsula Dr. off Seven Hills Rd., Traverse City, 231-223-7615.*

Chateau Chantal: Catch breathtaking vistas of both east and west Grand Traverse Bay from this 65-acre winery just north of Mapleton. Owned by former priest Robert Begin and his wife Natalie, a former nun, they named the winery after their daughter, Chantal. The European-style chateau, which sits atop one of the highest points on Old Mission Peninsula, is its tasting and touring building as well as a B&B inn. The winery produces a wide variety of award-winning varieties including Chardonnay, Riesling, Pinot Noir, Gewürztraminer, Merlot and Pinot Menier, as well as sparkling and ice wines. Wine seminars are held throughout the year. Open year-round. *15900 Rue de Vin, Traverse City, 231-223-4110.*

Chateau Grand Traverse: Find more spectacular views of water from its large tasting room set in the middle of more than 100 acres of vineyards. Noted for its excellent Rieslings, Chardonnays (both barrel fermented and "unwooded") and reds, including Merlot, Menier and Cabernet Franc, it also produces a variety of fruit wines. The wines regularly win state, national and international awards. *12239 Center Rd, 7 miles north of Traverse City on M 37, 231-223-7355.*

Peninsula Cellars: The tasting room, in a restored 19th-century Maple Grove Schoolhouse, offers handcrafted Rieslings, Chardonnay, Raftshol Red, Pinot Noir, and cherry and apple wines. Open May-November. *11480 Center Rd., southeast corner of Center and Carroll, 7 miles north of Traverse City on M 37, 231-223-4050.*

# Section Three

# My Fave Foodie Spots
# by Location

# MY FAVE FOODIE SPOTS BY LOCATION

## ACME

American Spoon Foods, Grand Traverse Resort, 100 Grand Traverse Village Blvd., 231-938-5358.

Amon Orchards, 8066 US 31 N, 800-937-1644 or 231-938-9160.

Trillium in the Grand Traverse Resort and Spa, 100 Grand Traverse Village Blvd., 231-938-2100 or 800-748-0303.

## ALDEN

Crystal Club, 9160-9166 Helena Rd., Alden, 231-331-6164.

## BAY HARBOR

The Galley Gourmet, 4181 Main St., 231-439-2668.

Latitude, 795 Front St., 231-439-2750.

Sagamore's, The Inn at Bay Harbor, 3600 Village Harbor Dr., 231-439-4059, 800-GO-BOYNE.

## BELLAIRE

Lulu's Bistro, 213 N. Bridge St., 231-533-5252.

Whispers in the Lodge at Cedar River, Shanty Creek, 800-678-4111.

## BEULAH

L'Chayim Deli, 274 S. Benzie Blvd., 231-882-5221.

Cherry Hut: 246 US 31, 231-882-4431.

Timmerin at The Inn at Beulah Beach, 173 Lake St., 231-882-5523.

## BOYNE CITY

Red Mesa Grill, 117 Water St., 231-582-0049.

## BUCKLEY

Punzel's, 8720 County Rd. 633, 231-263-7427.

## CEDAR

Pleva's Meats, 8974 S. Kasson St., 231-228-5000.

## CADILLAC

Hermann's European Café, 214 N. Mitchell St., 231-775-9563.

Marina Ristorante, 2404 Sunnyside Dr., 231-775-9322.

Terrace Room, McGuire's Resort, between M-115 and U.S. 131, 231-775-9947.

## CHARLEVOIX

American Spoon Foods, 315 Bridge St., 231-547-5222
Grey Gables, 308 Belvedere St., 231-547-9261.
Mahogany's Fine Dining, Charlevoix Country Club, 9600
    Clubhouse Dr., 231-547-3555.
Whitneys Oyster Bar, 307 Bridge St., 231-547-0818.

## ELK RAPIDS

Pearl's New Orleans Kitchen, 617 Ames St., 231-264-0530.

## ELLSWORTH

DeKorne Apiary, 10758 Essex Rd., 231-588-6062.
Rocky Top Farms, Essex Rd., 800-862-9303 or 231-599-2251.
The Rowe, 6303 Lake St., 866-432-5873 or 231-588-7351.
Tapawingo, 9502 Lake St., 231-588-7971.

## EMPIRE

Joe's Friendly Tavern, 11015 Front St., 231-326-5506.
The Manitou, M22 between Empire and Frankfort, 231-882-4761.

## FRANKFORT

Coho Café, 320 Main St., 231-352-6053.
Dinghy's Restaurant & Bar, 417 Main St., 231-352-4702.
Rhonda's Wharfside Inn, 300 Main St., 231-352-5300.

## ELBERTA

Elberta Beach Diner, 735 Frankfort Ave., 231-352-5273.
Trick Dog Gallery/Café, M-22 into Elberta, right on Furnace Rd.
along the bay, about a mile down,  231-352-TDOG.

## GRAWN

Rico's Café, 5790 US 31 South, 2 miles west of Chum's Corner,
    231-276-7070.

## HARBOR SPRINGS

American Spoon Foods, 245 East Main St., 231-526-8628.
The Fish, State Rd. (C77) at Stutsmanville Rd., 231-526-3969.

## HILLMAN

Thunder Bay Resort, on M32, 1-800-729-9375.

## INTERLOCHEN
Hofbrau, 2784 M 137, 231-276-6979.

## GLEN ARBOR
Art's Tavern, 6487 W. Western Ave. (M22), 231-334-3754.
Cherry Republic, 6026 S. Lake St., 800-206-6949.
Leelanau Coffee Roasting Co., 6443 Western Ave. (M22), 800-424-JAVA.
The Good Harbor Grill, 6584 Western Ave. (M22), 231-334-3555.

## KALKASKA
Shetler's Amazing Graze Farm, 5436 Tyler Rd., 6 miles east of Kalkaska off M-72, 231-258-8216.

## LAKE LEELANAU
Boskydel Vineyards, 7501 E. Otto Rd., 231-256-7272.
Chateau Fontaine, 2290 S. French Road on the west side of Lake Leelanau, 231-256-0000.
Dick's Pour House, 103 W. Phillips, 231-256-9912.
Good Harbor Vineyards, 34 S. Manitou Trail off M22, three miles south of Leland, 231-256-7165.
Kejara's Bridge, 302 W. Main St., 231-256-7720.
Key to the County, 104 Main St., 231-256-5397.
Harbor Hill Fruit Farm: 1742 Schomberg Rd., 3 miles south of Leland, 231-256-7666.

## LELAND
Stone House Bread, 407 S. Main St., 800-252-3218 or 231-256.2577.
Leland Cherry Co., 106 Lake St., Suite 2, 800-939-3199, 231-256-2033.
The Bluebird Restaurant & Bar, 101 River Street, 231-256-9081.
The Riverside Inn, 302 River St., 888-257-0102 or 231-256-9971.

## MANISTEE
Pleasanton Brick Oven Bakery, Manistee County, 231-864-2203.
Salt City Café, 50 Filer Street, Suite D, 231-398-9343.
Four Forty West, 440 W. River St., 231-723-7902.

## NORTHPORT
Fischer's Happy Hour Tavern, On M22 between Northport and
    Leland, 231-386-9923.
Kilcherman's Christmas Cove Farm, 11573 N. Kilcherman Rd.,
    231-386-5637.

## ONEKAMA
The Blue Slipper Bistro, 8058 1st St. on the corner, 231-889-4045.
Creative Expressions Café and Deli, 4857 Main St., 231-889-4236.

## PETOSKEY
Andante, 321 Bay St., 231-348-3321.
American Spoon Foods, 411 East Lake St., 231-347-1739.
American Spoon Gelato Café, 413 East Lake St., 231-347-7004.
Bear River Brewing Company, 317 E. Lake St., 231-348-7700.
Chandler's, 215-1/2 Howard St., 231-347-2981.
City Park Grill, 432 East Lake St., 231-347-0101.
Crooked Tree Breadworks, 2264 M119 Suite 5, 888-591-8688.
Kilwin's, 355 N. Division Rd., 231-347-3800.
Roast & Toast, 309 E. Lake St., 231-347-7767.
The H. O. Rose Room, Stafford's Perry Hotel, Bay and Lewis streets,
    800-737-1899.
Stafford's Bay View Inn, 2011 Woodland Ave. off US-31 North,
    Petoskey, 231-347-2771, 800-258-1886.
Villa il Ristorante Italiano, US 131 S, 231-347-1440.

## SUTTONS BAY
Black Star Farms, 10844 E. Revold Rd., Suttons Bay, 231-271-4884.
Café Bliss, 420 St. Josephs, 231-271-5000.
Boone's Primetime Pub, St. Josephs, 231-271-6688.
Busha's Brae Herb Farm, by appointment only, 231-271-6284.
Chateau de Leelanau, 5048 S. West Bay Shore Dr., 231-271-8888.
Ciccone Vineyard & Winery, 10343 E. Hilltop Rd., 231-271-5551.
Covered Wagon Farm Market, 8996 M-204 (also known as E. Duck
    Lake Rd.), 231-271-6658.
Flying Scotts' Farm, M-204, 231-271-3871.
45th Parallel Café, 102 S. Broadway, 231-271-2233.
Hansen Foods, 91 4th Street, 231-271-4280.
Hattie's, 111 St. Josephs St., 231-271-6222.
Leelanau Cheese Co., 10844 E. Revold Rd., 231-271-2600.
L. Mawby Vineyards, 4519 S. Elm Valley Rd., 231-271-3522.

Raftshol Vineyards Inc., 1865 N. West Bay Shore Dr., 231-271-5650.
Shady Lane Cellars, 9580 Shady Lane, 231-947-8865.
Silvertree, 305 N. St. Josephs, 231-271-2271.
Willow Vineyards, 10702 East Hilltop Rd., 231-271-4810.

TRAVERSE CITY
American Spoon Foods, 230 East Front St., 231-935-4480.
(La Cuisine) Amical, 229 E. Front St., 231-941-8888.
Apache Trout Grill, 13671 S. W. Bay Shore Dr., 231-947-7079.
Auntie Pasta's, at Logan's Landing, 2030 South Airport Rd.,
    231-941-8147.
Bardon's Ice Cream, 1100 E. Front, 231-941-4326.
Bay Bread Company, 601 Randolph St. at Maple, 231-922-8022.
Benjamin Twiggs, 1215 E. Front St., 877-236-8944.
Blue Goat Wine Shop, 875 E. Front St., 231-941-9463.
The Boathouse, 14039 Peninsula Dr. in Bowers Harbor, 231-223-4030.
Boone's Long Lake Inn, 7208 Secor Rd., 231-946-3991.
Bowers Harbor Inn, 13512 Peninsula Drive, 231-223-4222.
The Bowery, 13512 Peninsula Dr., 231-223-4333.
Brady's Bar, 401 S. Union St., 231-946-8153.
Bubba's, 223 W. Grandview Parkway, 231-995-0570.
Burritt's Market, 509 W. Front St., 231-946-3300.
The Cajun Bayou, 810 E. Front St., 231-933-3300.
Carlson's Fish Market, 511 W. Front St., 231- 941-9392.
Cherry Stop, 211 E. Front St., 800-286-7209, 231-929-3990.
China Buffet King, 1112 S. Garfield, 231-933-9999.
City Kitchen, 826 W. Front St., 231-932-2201.
Dairy Bar, behind the Mackinaw Brewing Co. at Front and Cass,
    231-933-1100.
Dairy Lodge, Dairy Lodge, 405 N. Division, 231-941-4374.
Dairy Queen, 3200 S. Airport, 231-935-4333;
    1660 U.S. 31 N., 231-938-0441.
Dill's Olde Towne Saloon, 423 S. Union, 231-947-7534.
Don's Drive-In, 2030 U.S. 31 N., 231-938-1860.
Fieldstone Deli, 7270 N. Long Lake Rd., 231-922-7712.
Folgarelli's, 424 W. Front St., 231-941-7651.
Gordie Howe's Tavern & Eatery, 851 S. Garfield near Hastings,
    231-929-4693.
Grand Traverse Pie Co., 525 W. Front St., 231-922-7437.
Green House Café, 115 E. Front St., 231-929-SOUP (7687).

Horizon Books Shine Café, 245 E. Front St., 231-946-7290.
Kilwin's Chocolates, 129 E. Front, 231-946-2403.
The Left Bank Café, 120 Park, 231-929-9060.
Mary's Kitchen Port, 539 W. Front St., 231-941-0525.
Maxbauer's Meats, 407 S. Union St. in Olde Towne, 231-947-7698.
Mode's Bum Steer, 125 E. State St., 231-947-9832.
Moomers Homemade Ice Cream, 7263 N. Long Lake Rd.,
      231-941-4122.
Mr. Mike's Detroit Pizza, 920 U.S. 31N, 231-922-7141.
Mustard's, 202 E. State St., 231-929-0700.
North Peak Brewery, 400 W. Front St., 231- 941-7325.
Northwestern Michigan College, Oleson Center, 1701 E. Front St.,
      231-995-1196.
North Peak Brewing Company, 400 W. Front St., 231-941-7325.
Old Mission Tavern, 17015 Center Rd., 231-223-7280.
Paesano's Pizza, 447 E. Front St., 231-941-5740.
The Peninsula Grill, 14091 Center Rd., 231-223-7200.
Poppycock's, 128 E. Front St., 231-941-7632.
Ray's Coffeehouse, 129 E. Front St., 231-929-1006.
Reflections Restaurant and Lounge, Waterfront Inn Resort Hotel,
2061 US 31 N, 231-938-1100 or 1-800-551-9283.
The Riverside Café, 439 E. Front St., 231-932-0529.
Silver Swan, 13692 SW Bay Shore Dr., 231-932-0203.
Sleder's Family Tavern, 717 Randolph St., 231-947-9213.
The Suncatcher, at Cherryland Airport, 1330 Airport Access Rd.,
      231-941-0192.
Taqueria Margarita, 1319 W. South Airport Rd., 231-935-3712.
T.C. Hunan Chinese Restaurant, 1425 S. Airport Rd. in the 42$^{nd}$ St.
      Plaza, 231-947-1388.
TC Traders, 1796 S. Garfield, 231-929-9885.
Underground Cheesecake Co., 406 S. Union St., 231-929-4418.
Wine Country Market,  541 W. Front St., 231-935-17768.
Windows, 7677 SW Bay Shore Dr., 231-941-0100.

WILLIAMSBURG
Engle Ridge Farm, 6754 Yuba Rd., Williamsburg, 888-448-5817.

# Index

## Good Taste

# Index

A

American Spoon Foods, 143
American Spoon Gelato Café 145
Amical 10
Amon Orchards 143, 149
Andante 12
Apache Trout Grill 13
Arcadia Bluffs 14
Art's Tavern 137
Auntie Pasta's 15

B

Bardon's 152
Bay Bread Co. 136
Becasse 16 (see La Becasse)
Bel Lago Vineyards and Winery 159
Benjamin Twiggs 143
Bibb's Manitou Market 149 (see Manitou Market)
Black Star Farms 139, 159
The Bluebird Restaurant & Bar 18
The Blue Goat 156
Blue Slipper Bistro 20
The Boathouse 22
Boone's Long Lake Inn 137
Boone's Primetime 137
Boskydel Vineyards 159
Bowers Harbor Inn 24
Bowers Harbor Vineyards 161
The Bowery 26
Brady's Bar 137
Brownwood Acres 143
Bubba's 28
Buchan's Blueberry Hill 149
Burritt's Market 155
Busha's Brae Herb Farm 149

C

Café Bliss 30
Cajun Bayou 31
Carlson's Fish Market 155
Chandler's 33
Chateau Chantal 161

Chateau de Leelanau 159
Chateau Fontaine 159
Chateau Grand Traverse: 161
L' Chayim Deli 145
Cherry Hut 143, 145, 157
Cherry Republic 143
Cherry Stop 143
China Buffet King 34
Chrissy's Farm Market 149
Ciccone Vineyard & Winery 159
City Kitchen 35
City Park Grill 37
Coho Café 38
Covered Wagon Farm Market 149
Creative Expressions 40
Crooked Tree Breadworks 136
Crystal Club 42

D

Dairy Lodge 153
Dairy Queen 153
Dan's Market and Garden Center 149
DeKorne Apiary 149
Dick's Pour House 137
Dill's Olde Towne Saloon 44
Dinghy's Restaurant & Bar 46
Don's Drive-In 137

E

Elberta Beach Diner 48
Elzer Farm 150
Engle Ridge Farm 143

F

Fieldstone Deli 145, 158
Fischer's Happy Hour Tavern 138
The Fish 49
Flying Scotts' Farm 150
Folgarelli's 154
45th Parallel Cafe 51
Four-Forty West 52
Friske Orchard 150
Funistrada 53

G

Gallagher's Farm Market 150
Galley Gourmet 55
Gibby's Fries 141

Glen Brown's Fruit Stand  150
The Good Harbor Grill  56
Good Harbor Vineyards  160
Gordie Howe's Tavern  58
Grand Traverse Pie Company  157
Green House Cafe  60
Grey Gables  62

H

Hansen Foods  155
Harbor Hill Fruit Farm  150
Hattie's  63
Hermann's European Café & Inn  64
Hofbrau  65
Horizon Books Shine Café  146

J

Joe's Friendly Tavern  138

K

Kejara's Bridge  67
Key to the County  69
Kilcherman's Christmas Cove Farm,  143
Kilwin's  153
Kilwin's Chocolate factory  144
King's Orchards  150

L

L. Mawby Vineyards  160
La Becasse  16 (see Becasse)
Latitude  71
Leelanau Cheese Co.  139
Leelanau Coffee Roasting Co.  146
Leelanau Country Inn  72
Leelanau Farmers' Markets  150
Leelanau Wine Cellars  160
The Left Bank Cafe  74
Leland Cherry Co.  143
Lighthouse Market  150
Lulu's Bistro  76

M

Mahogany's  78
Manitou  79
Manitou Market  149
Marina Ristorante  80
Mary's Kitchen Port  156

Maxbauer's Meats  156
Mode's Bum Steer 82
Moomers  152
Moose Drool Coffee 142
Mountain Spuds  141
Mr. Mike's Detroit Pizza  158
Mustard's  146

N

The New York  84
North Peak Brewing Co. 88, 138
Northwestern Michigan College  86

O

Old Mission Tavern  89
Omena U-Pick Cut Flowers  150

P

Paesano's Pizza  158
Pearl's New Orleans Kitchen  91
Peninsula Cellars  161
The Peninsula Grill  93
Pleasanton Brick Oven Bakery  136
Pleva's Meats  156
Poppycock's  95
Punzel's  97

R

Raftshol Vineyards Inc  160
Ray's Coffeehouse  146
Red Mesa Grill  98
Reflections Restaurant and Lounge  99
Rhonda's Wharfside Inn 100
Rico's Café  138, 158
The Riverside Café  102
Riverside Inn  104
The Roadhouse Mexican Bar & Grill  105
Roast & Toast  146
Rocky Top Farms  143
Rose Room  107
The Rowe  108

S

Sagamore's  109
Salt City Café  146
Shady Lane Cellars  160
Shetler's Family Dairy  148

Silver Swan 147
Silvertree 147
Sleder's Family Tavern 110
Stafford's Bay View Inn 112
Stone House Bread 136
The Suncatcher 138

T

Tapawingo 113
Taqueria Margarita 115
TC Hunan 117
TC Traders 138
Terrace Room 118
Thunder Bay Resort 121
Timmerin 119
Traverse City Farmer's Market 151
Trick Dog Gallery/Café 147
Trillium 123

U

Underground Cheesecake Co. 140

V

Villa il Ristorante Italiano 125

W

Walloon Lake Inn 128
Whispers 129
Wildflower 131
Willow Vineyards 160
Windows 133
Wine Country Market 156